God Is Great

Interactive Bible Stories
for Families

First and Second Grades

Volume 2

DPI
DISCIPLESHIP
PUBLICATIONS
INTERNATIONAL

God Is Great, Volume 2

Printed in the United States of America

*Edited by Vickie Boone, Amby Murphy and Dede Petre
Cover design: Chad Crossland and Tony Bonazzi
Illustrator: Edgar Walcott
Interior design: Thais Gloor and Christine Nolan*

ISBN: 1-57782-164-5

Dedication

Even though Amby Murphy contributed to this book, we at DPI wanted to surprise her by dedicating it to her. She is tireless and visionary in her commitment to the children in the kingdom. She infused every page of the first and second grade curriculum with fun and creativity—she enjoyed working on it as much as the children enjoy using it. Thank you, Amby.

Acknowledgments

We would like to thank Jo-Ann Austin, Kim Caminos, Linda Howard, Catherine Paul and all of the other volunteers in the San Diego Church of Christ for their undying dedication to the Kingdom Kids Curriculum. Their tireless efforts, deep faith and creative minds brought the 1st and 2nd grade curriculum to life.

Contents

Foreword

It is my privilege to write the foreword for this much-needed book. When we began thinking about developing our own Kingdom Kids Curriculum back in 1995, I only partially realized the significance of what we were doing. Certainly anyone who is spiritually minded can see the value of such a prescribed course of study for our children, but I doubt that any of us really understands how vital it is to our families.

While we were working on the curriculum, my grown son said something to me that heightened my understanding considerably: "Dad, I am not sure if I would have stayed in the spiritual battle were it not for the amount of Bible I learned as a young person in Bible classes. I simply know too much of God's word to ever leave the church."

All parents would be struck emotionally upon hearing such a statement from their child. What if Bryan had not attended those classes? What if those teachers had not poured themselves into communicating the divine message to him? What if we, as parents, had not concentrated on teaching the Bible in the home? Instead of being thrilled with where our two children and their mates are spiritually, we would be filled with heartache and remorse. And now that grandchildren are coming along, we are even more grateful for all that we and others did to train Bryan and Renee in the Lord's principles.

As important as our children's ministry may be at church, what we do as parents is more important. The Proverb writer said it well:

> Train a child in the way he should go,
> and when he is old he will not turn from it.
> (Proverbs 22:6)

We must see the children's ministry as a supplement to what we are doing in the home. We as parents must have a God-driven desire to embrace the opportunity and responsibility that is ours in helping our children get to heaven. As an elder who has seen many children of disciples do great as adults and many others do terribly, I cannot over-emphasize the importance of our role as parents in training our children.

The goal of the curriculum is to teach God's heart to our children and help them to grow into strong spiritual adults. The goal of this book is to help you, as parents, to take full advantage of the curriculum and reinforce it in your homes.

God Is Great, Volume 2 is designed to help you reach your child's heart. In it you will find interactive Bible stories, fun pages, scripture memory activities and "act it out" pages—all reflecting the Biblical themes of the curriculum. It is one of the finest tools available to bring you and your child together in the presence of Jesus. I commend it fully to you, and I urge you to use this and all other such tools to help the message of God become deeply embedded in your child's heart.

May we all one day meet at God's throne, rejoicing in the fact that we as families have fought the good fight of faith together and have been victorious by the grace of our loving Father! And to him be the glory!

Gordon Ferguson
September 2001

Introduction

Welcome to Kingdom Kids at Home, a bridge between the curriculum in the classroom and your child's heart at home.

This book has been developed to connect you to the valuable learning that occurs in the children's ministry. We want to give you tools to reinforce the concepts of the Kingdom Kids Curriculum in your home. Family time ideas, prayer ideas, crafts, fun pages and scripture memory activities will help you to nurture the faith planted in your child's heart.

Our hope is that you will use this book together with your child to help bring the Bible to life. Your child will love to spend special time with you as together you have fun learning about God. Read, color, act, sing and create!

God Is Great, Volume 2 has been written with your 1st and 2nd grader in mind. The Parent Pages are designed to help you stimulate your child's spiritual thinking through discussion, crafts and prayer times together. The Brain Food pages give you many creative ways to help your child put God's word in his heart. The Fun Pages can be done independently by your child, though he may prefer for you to help him. The Act It Out pages are best done with several "actors" and can be used during family time.

The Kingdom Kids Curriculum is divided into eight quarters, presented over a two-year period. Each quarter contains several units on various topics. Year two of the 1st and 2nd grade curriculum is made up of ten units. Each chapter in this book corresponds to one unit and is designed to reinforce the Bible lessons presented in class. See the appendix for a detailed outline of the second year of Bible class lessons.

Your enthusiasm and animation will bring the Bible to life, and God will reward your desire to impress his word upon your child. Let the Spirit move, and be assured that you and your child will have many exciting adventures while creating special family memories.

> These commandments that I give you today are to be upon your hearts. Impress them on your children. Talk about them when you sit at home and when you walk along the road, when you lie down and when you get up.
>
> *Deuteronomy 6:6-7*

God's Great Book

In Bible Class

Psalm 46; 2 Timothy 3; Romans 15; Hebrews 1; Matthew 7; John 14,15,20; Ephesians 2

Here your child will explore God's plan to give us the Bible. These lessons look at how God spoke through the apostles and prophets to give us the Old and New Testaments. Your child will learn that God not only speaks, but he listens too! These lessons will help your child to think of ways to use God's words every day.

Bringing It Home

In this chapter:

- Talk about God's words being a foundation.
- Search for important words hidden in a puzzle.
- Find the missing New Testament books on the Bible train.
- Learn about the wise and foolish builders.
- Discover true and false statements from the Bible.
- Act out being a modern-day prophet.

Just for Fun

- Visit a construction site and observe a new foundation. Explain to your child the importance of laying a solid foundation beneath any building. Ask your child why he thinks it is important to not allow cracks or holes in the foundation. Help him to make the connection between this and Jesus' parable in Matthew 7:24-27 of the wise and foolish builders.
- Visit a museum of ancient history (or a library) to look at ancient artifacts dating back to Bible times. Even better, find out if there are any disciples who can give you a knowledgeable tour. Explain that the Bible is a true and historic document that was written by people who lived at the same time as some of the items you see in the museum. Encourage your child by sharing some basic facts about the Bible's historical accuracy. Let your child see how excited you are with these facts and how they have helped your faith.
- Make a list of Bible ABCs as a family. Write out the alphabet and then next to each letter write a statement or word that describes a truth or benefit we see in the Bible.

Pages

God-Breathed

2 Timothy 3:16-17

Read this passage to your child and talk about the importance of listening to God's words. Explain that God's words are always useful for helping us to do what is right.

Questions:

- What is an example of something useful? What is it useful for?
- What are some ways that the Bible is useful to our family?
- How do you feel when you are well-prepared for a trip or a project at school?
- How does it make you feel to know that God wants to "equip" or prepare you to do good things?

Bring It to Life!

At the beginning of a day, give every member of your family (except small children) a small "tool" or tool-shaped item to carry in their pockets as a reminder that God's words can help them throughout the day. At the end of the day, talk about ways that God's words were useful.

Bring It to God!

Pray together for God to help your family love the Bible and to find ways to use it every day. Thank God for the ways that his word helped you throughout the week.

Family Times

Like a Rock

Matthew 7:24-27

Read this passage and ask your child to describe what happened to both of the builders.

Questions:

- What are some things that make us upset or afraid? Explain that these are the "storms" described by Jesus in this passage.
- Which builder had a storm beat against his house? Explain that both builders experienced storms but only one house survived.
- Ask your child if he can think of a time when your faith helped you during a difficult situation.

Bring It to Life!

Find a large, smooth rock on which you can write (or paint) the words, "The Wise Man Built His House on the Rock," and put it where everyone can see it and be reminded of Jesus' teaching.

Bring It to God!

Think of some difficult situations that you or your child are facing and pray specifically for God to help you "stand up" in the midst of each storm. Thank God for the ways that he has already brought your family through storms.

Brain Food

Have fun playing these games to learn and memorize feature scriptures.

Bubbling Over

All scripture is God-breathed.
2 Timothy 3:16

What You'll Need
- a bottle of bubbles with wand

Blow some bubbles and try to say the verse as many times as you can before the last bubble pops. Take turns blowing bubbles. For a more challenging activity, include verse 17 in this activity. Help your child to appreciate the idea that "when God talks, people should listen," which is why you want to listen to God's words.

Building Blocks

"Everyone who hears these things I say and obeys them is like a wise man. The wise man built his house on rock. "
Matthew 7:24 (ICV)

What You'll Need
- 24 building blocks or interlocking puzzle pieces

Using the blocks, practice saying the verse, placing one block for each word until the verse and reference are complete. (There is one block included for the reference.) For a more visual activity, write each word directly onto a block (or a piece of tape on the block) to help your child place them in the correct order.

God Is Great

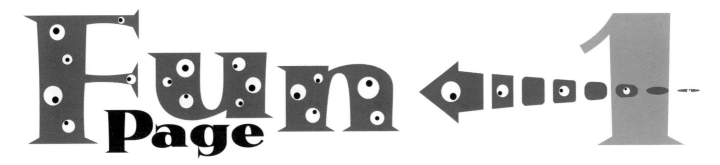

Fun Page 1

Instructions

Find and circle the words below.

learn	scriptures
read	Bible
Jesus	apostles
prophet	obey
remember	God-breathed

```
S L E A R N D G P R Z
H C U W E K P D Z O R
X I G J A W R L S F E
Y O E J D K O Q E B M
R C K D J A P C R L E
S U S E J N H C U E M
C K D O E X E K T M B
Z Y J L Q S T H P B E
H T B Q K G S D I R R
V I F K O B E Y R L D
B T M S Y L E Z C P T
S A P O S T L E S X I
G O D B R E A T H E D
```

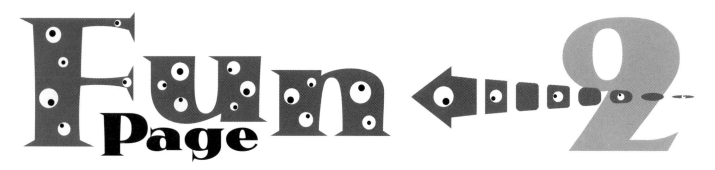

Instructions

The train below contains the names of the books of the New Testament in their correct Biblical order.
Can you fill in the seven missing books? You may need to look in the Bible to find the correct spelling.

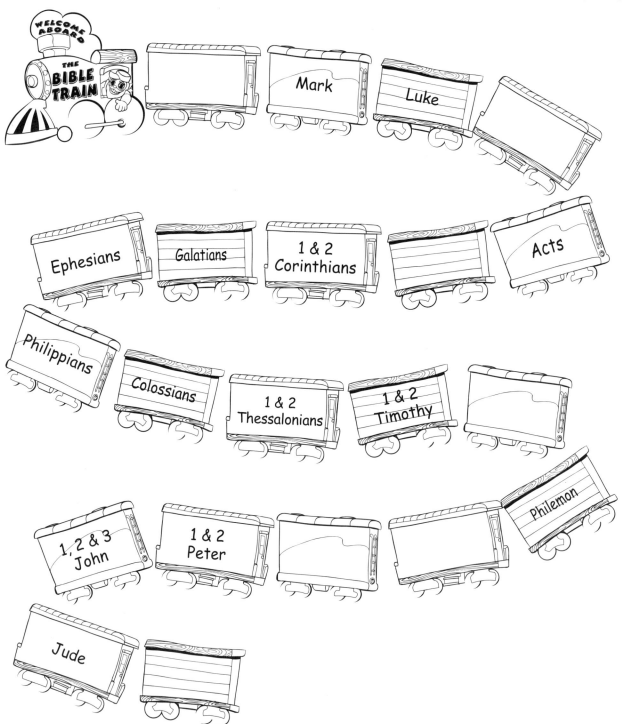

God Is Great

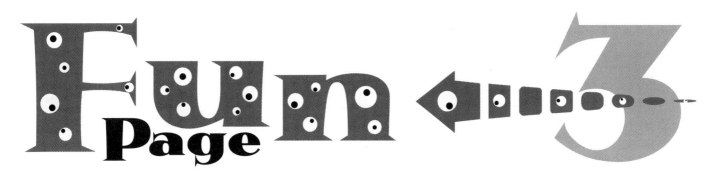

Instructions

The scripture, Hebrews 1:1 (ICV), is all mixed-up below. Number the boxes in the right order so that the verse can be read correctly.

He spoke to them

In the past

different ways.

and in many

many times

through the prophets.

God spoke to our ancestors

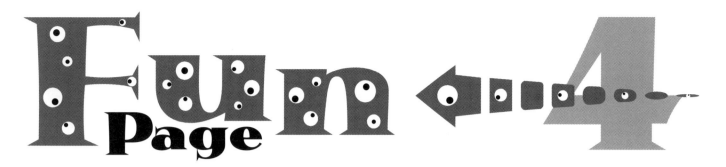

Instructions

Draw a line from the Bible to the true statements that we learn from the Bible. There are three statements that are not based on the Bible.

Jesus is Lord.

God created the world.

God loves pizza.

God keeps his promises.

God likes to sleep.

Jesus likes to climb trees.

God is love.

God protects me.

God Is Great

Act It Out

God spoke to the prophets in many different ways and at various times. Sometimes they were in the middle of doing something when God spoke to them.

Imagine...

that you are a modern-day prophet and God is speaking to you.

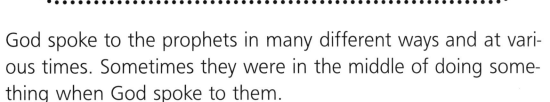

Act It Out!

What is going to be the message God wants you to tell the people? Who are you going to tell?

Props

a bath robe or sheet
(to dress like a prophet)
anything else necessary for your skit

Answer Key

pg 13

```
S  L  E  A  R  N  D  G  P  R  Z
H  C  U  W  E  K  P  D  Z  O  R
X  I  G  J  A  W  R  L  S  F  E
Y  O  E  J  D  K  O  Q  E  B  M
R  C  K  D  J  A  P  C  R  L  E
S  U  S  E  J  N  H  C  U  E  M
C  K  D  O  E  X  E  K  T  M  B
Z  Y  J  L  Q  S  T  H  P  B  E
H  T  B  Q  K  G  S  D  I  R  R
V  I  F  K  O  B  E  Y  R  L  D
B  T  M  S  Y  L  E  Z  C  P  T
S  A  P  O  S  T  L  E  S  X  I
G  O  D  B  R  E  A  T  H  E  D
```

pg 14 Matthew, John, Romans, Titus, Hebrews, James, Revelation

pg 16

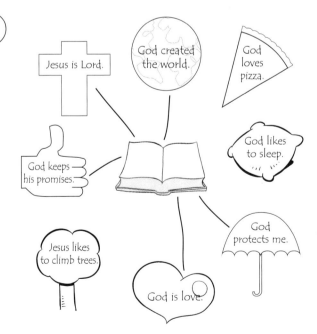

God's Great Disciples

Parent

In Bible Class

Matthew 18; Luke 5, 9, 11, 15; John 3; Acts 2

Your child will travel with Jesus and his followers while imagining Jesus teaching them about prayer and depending on God. Through these lessons, your child will see God's power at work in Peter's life as well as in the life of the prodigal son. In the end, your child will learn about baptism and the faith-filled decisions that lead up to it. Your child will be encouraged to consider her own future as a disciple one day.

Bringing It Home

In this chapter:

- Learn that Jesus loves bold prayers!
- Practice "fishing" and "seeing" as you memorize verses.
- Draw the results of Peter's obedience.
- Discuss being humble and why this is important.
- Solve a coded message about repentance.
- Pretend you are Peter in the boat.

Just for Fun

- Visit a farm and observe the pig sty or look up information about pigs and see what their lives are like. Talk with your child about Luke 15:11-32 and what it might have been like for the prodigal son to have to take care of the pigs.
- Make and decorate a family prayer chain. Cut out paper strips and write individual prayer needs for each person in your family. Then link them together using tape or a stapler. Customize the chain by selecting specific colors denoting individual needs (e.g., pink for Mommy, blue for Daddy, green for Jimmy) and one common color for general family needs. Hang the chain in a place where everyone can see it and pray through the chain during the week at meals and bedtimes.

Pages

Knock, Knock. Who's There?

Luke 11:1-10

Read this passage to your child. Explain that Jesus taught the importance of prayer to the disciples by telling them the story about the friends and the bread.

Questions:

- Reread verses 2-4 and discuss any words that are unfamiliar to your child.
- Why does God want his children to be bold in their prayers?
- How does it make you feel to know that God wants you to be bold and persistent in your prayers?
- What are some things that you are going to be more bold and persistent about in prayer?

Bring It to Life!

Share with your child about the boldest prayer(s) you ever prayed and how God answered you. Ask other disciples about their bold prayers and share these stories with your child.

Bring It to God!

Decide as a family to focus on one specific need that you will be bold and persistent about in your prayers. Watch how God works!

Family Times

Great Change!

Matthew 18:1-4

Read these chapters and recount them to your child in your own words. Emphasize how destructive selfishness can be. (For example, Esau's hunger, Rebekah's favoritism, Jacob's deceitfulness)

Questions:

- What do you think the word "humble" means?
- Who is an example of a humble person? What makes them so?
- How is a child humble?
- When is it the hardest for you to be humble? Why?

Bring It to Life!

Bring out baby pictures and/or videos of your child or yourself as babies. Point out that what makes babies so cute is their innocence and trust—the same things that God wants us to have in our hearts as his followers. Point out that young children don't get defensive or talk back when they are wrong. They don't blame others. They just live their lives totally dependent upon their parents (or caretakers) which is how God wants us to depend on him.

Bring It to God!

Have a family prayer in which each person "humbles" himself by asking for forgiveness from someone else and from God.

Brain Food

Have fun playing these games to learn and memorize feature scriptures.

Simon Says

"Master, we've worked hard all night and haven't caught anything. But because you say so, I will let down the nets."
Luke 5:5

What You'll Need
- a piece of netting or mesh
- many blocks or small stuffed animals

Explain to your child that Simon Peter was the one who spoke these words to Jesus. Take turns being "Simon Peter" and lead the rest of the family in saying the verse in an echo style. For example, you say, "Master" and then they repeat "Master." You say, "we've worked hard all night" and they repeat, etc. When you say the last part of the verse, take the netting and place it down on the floor or ground. Have the rest of the family put the blocks or animals on the netting to represent the fish. Fold the netting and pull it in. Repeat this activity until everyone has had a chance to be "Simon Peter."

New Eyes

"I tell you the truth, no one can see the kingdom of God unless he is born again."
John 3:3

What You'll Need
- a pair of sunglasses or dress-up glasses

Say the verse together several times. Then, go around in a circle saying the verse one word at a time with each person saying the next word. Place the glasses in the middle of your circle. The person who says the word "see" picks up the glasses and puts them on until the end of the verse. Then return the glasses to the middle of the circle for the next round.

God Is Great

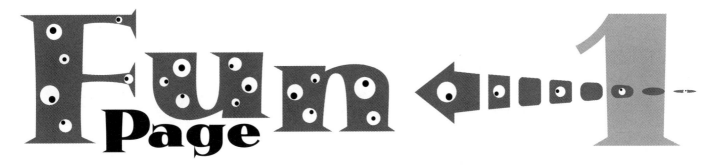

Fun Page 1

Instructions

In Luke 5:1-11, we see that Simon Peter obeyed Jesus even though he was tired and confused. Finish the picture by drawing Jesus and Simon Peter in the boat. Be sure to have Simon Peter pulling on the net. In the net draw many, many fish to show how God blessed Simon Peter's obedience.

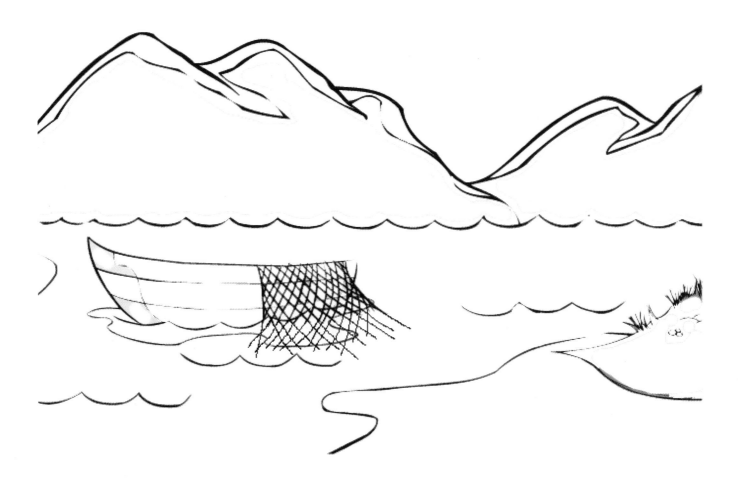

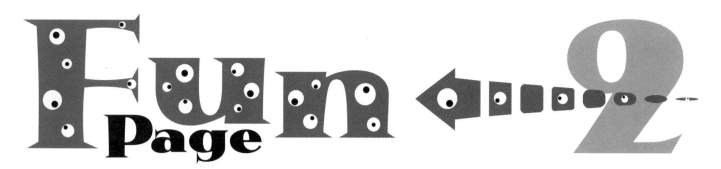

Instructions

Draw a green circle around the pictures of things that you pray about every day.
Draw a blue line under the pictures of things that you can be thankful for every day.
Draw a red circle around the pictures of things that show when you need to pray for God's help.

God Is Great

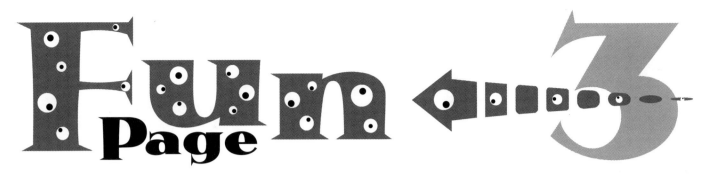

Instructions

Answer the question by using the key to fill in the blanks below.

R 🏜 P 🏜 👁 T ✔ 👁 C 🏜 M 🏜 ✔ 👁 S

_ _ _ _ _ _ _ _ _ _ _

CH ✔ 👁 G 🏴 👁 G Y 👂 📢 R M 🏴 👁 D

_ _ _ _ _ _ _ _ _ _ _ _

✔ 👁 D Y 👂 📢 R ✔ CT 🏴 👂 👁 S

_ _ _ _ _ _ _ _ _ _

T 👂 PL 🏜 ✔ S 🏜 G 👂 D.

_ _ _ _ _ _ _ _

Key Code

A = ✔   O = 👂
E = 🏜   U = 📢
I = 🏴   N = 👁

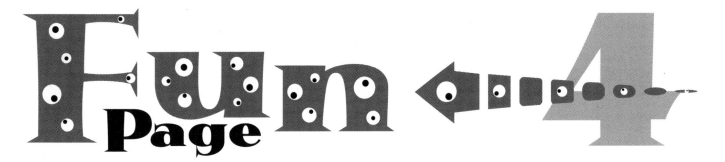

Instructions

Find the hidden letters to describe what is happening here in the picture. Write the letters in the spaces below. Color the picture.

_ _ _ _ _ _ _ _ _

God Is Great

Act It Out

God showed Peter that Jesus could really make things happen when he caused Peter to bring in all those fish after not catching anything all night.

Imagine...

Pretend that you are Peter with the disciples in the boat.

Act It Out!

Act out the scene of the nighttime fishing trip without Jesus and the daytime fishing trip with Jesus.

Props

couch or bed for a boat
blanket for a net
many fish (stuffed animals or blocks)
outfits for fishermen

Answer Key

pg 25 — Repentance means changing your mind and your actions to please God.

pg 26 — BAPTISM

God Is Great

God's Great Church

Parent

In Bible Class

John 13; Matthew 5,18; Hebrews 13; 1 Corinthians 12

Your child is making some exciting discoveries about the church—it is *not* a building but a very special group of people! He will see Jesus' standards for love and resolving conflict as he learns that Jesus wants his best friends to be in the church. Your child is being introduced to the concept of the body of Christ. He is learning that God has carefully chosen men and women to lead the church so that everyone in the church will be strong in their faith and in their relationships with God and each other.

Bringing It Home

In this chapter:

Talk about how Jesus showed his love.
Memorize scriptures while hopping and erasing.
- Finish a fun worksheet that describes how to resolve conflicts.
- Consider the leaders of your church and how to encourage them.
- Draw pictures of leaders.
- Act out ways to make your friends feel special.

Just for Fun

- Check out a book from the library on the human body. Be amazed at how the intricate systems in the human body work together so that we can do so many things. Help your child to understand that the church has been designed by God to work together in the same amazing ways so that through us, others will learn about Jesus.
- Choose a church leader and his family to encourage. Plan to bring a meal to them on a day when they have meetings or late appointments. Make up a fun "family quiz" for them to complete to find out their favorite things such as movies, foods, candy, games, teams, as well as birthdays and anniversaries. Ask them to fill out the "family quiz" as you drop off the dinner. Use this information in the future to encourage them again and again.
- Make a "Prayer and Pretzel" calendar for one month and pray as a family for different members of the church every day. Share the church prayer requests with your child so that he can feel a part of helping to pray for those needs. Prepare a small bag of pretzels (the traditional twisted shape) for people you've prayed for with a note to let them know they are in your prayers. NOTE: Pretzels were originally supposed to resemble praying hands.

God Is Great

Pages

Friends to the End

Hebrews 13:7

Read this passage and explain that Jesus said these words after he washed the disciples' feet—something that only servants normally did for their masters.

Questions:

- What are some ways that Jesus showed his love to his disciples? Make a list.
- What are some ways that we can show love to our friends today like Jesus did?
- What did Jesus say would happen if we love others like he loved us?

Bring It to Life!

Find a space on a wall or door to mount a large piece of corkboard or similar material. Dedicate this area for pictures of "kingdom friends" including children and families from churches around the world. Take time to look at the pictures and remember special times with them. Think of ways to stay in touch with friends who live far away.

Bring It to God!

Make a decision to pray every day for friends who are not in the church. Pray with your child to be able to show Jesus' love to these friends so that they will want to come to church with your family.

Family Times

Follow the Leader

Hebrews 13:7

Read this verse to your child and ask him if there are any words he does not understand.

Questions:

- This verse tells us to remember our leaders. Can you think of some leaders in the church? What are their names and how do they lead in the ministry?
- This verse tells us to consider the outcome of their way of life. Can you describe one of these leaders? What are they like? How do they make you feel special? How have they helped your family?
- This verse tells us to imitate their faith. What is one way a leader has demonstrated great faith in your ministry. How can you do the same thing in your family?

Bring It to Life!

Explain to your child that Jesus is the "leader of leaders" because he was the greatest servant of all. Help your child to understand that leaders lead by serving others the way Jesus did. Think of some ways that your family can "lead" by serving another family this week.

Bring It to God!

Pray with your child for the leaders in your ministry, thanking God for them by name and asking God to help them in their different areas of service. NOTE: Be sure that your child knows who the main leaders are in your church and local ministry. If he does not, introduce your child to them at church or by making a special visit.

Brain Food

Have fun playing these games to learn and memorize feature scriptures.

Sock Hop

"If you love one another, everyone will know that you are my disciples."
John 13:35 (NIRV)

What You'll Need
• No additional materials

Say the verse together several times. Then, say the verse together while hopping up and down on two feet. Then, say the verse together while hopping on one foot and then again while hopping on the other foot. Take turns saying the verse one at a time while hopping. Make up fun variations with hopping and reciting the verse, such as: jump rope, eyes closed, to music, etc.

Vanishing Verse

Now you are the body of Christ, and each one of you is a part of it.
1 Corinthians 12:27

What You'll Need
• blackboard (or dry-erase board)
• chalk (or dry-erase marker)
• suitable eraser

Write the scripture memory verse and reference on the blackboard and say it together several times. Erase the first word and then say the entire verse and reference from memory. With each new turn, erase the next word, and then say the entire verse and reference from memory. Continue until you have erased the entire verse and reference and can say it completely from memory.

God Is Great

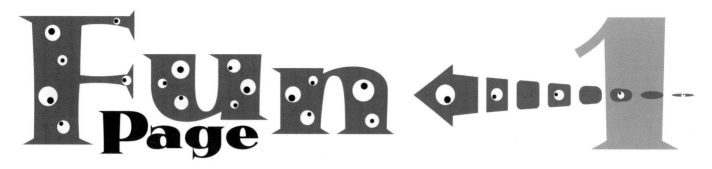

Instructions

Draw a line matching the phrase to the correct picture that shows how we can be like Jesus.

Greet others warmly because Jesus would greet me warmly.

Do helpful things for people because Jesus helps me.

Say kind things to others because Jesus is kind to me.

Pray for others because Jesus prayed for me.

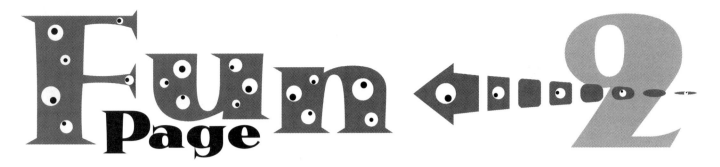

Instructions

Using the four words below, fill in the blanks of the phrases below each picture. Then color in the pictures.

Get help   problem   forgive   talk

When there is
a _____...

_____ about
it right away!

_____
if you need it.

Then _____
and have a great day!

God Is Great

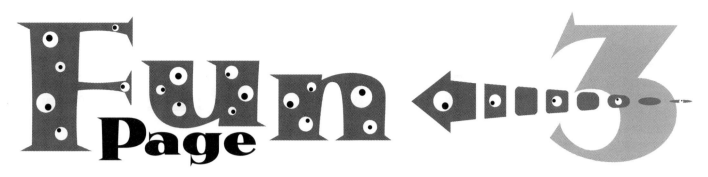

Instructions

Think of four leaders that God has put in your life and draw a picture of each one in the four frames below. You may want to draw only their heads and shoulders as the frames are small. Write their names below the pictures in the boxes provided.

Remember your leaders,
who spoke the word of God to you.
Hebrews 13:7

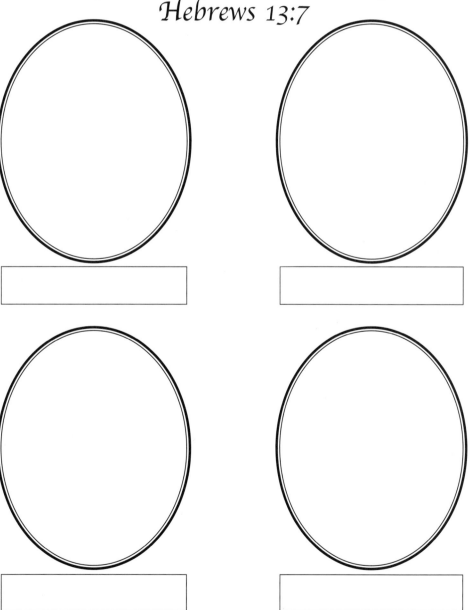

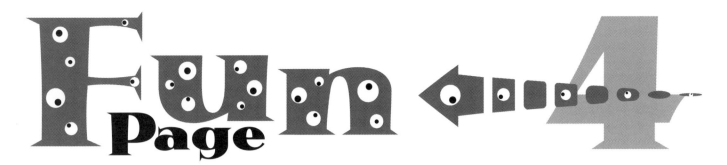

Instructions

The following pictures describe different ways we serve God. Draw a line from the picture to the words that match what is happening.

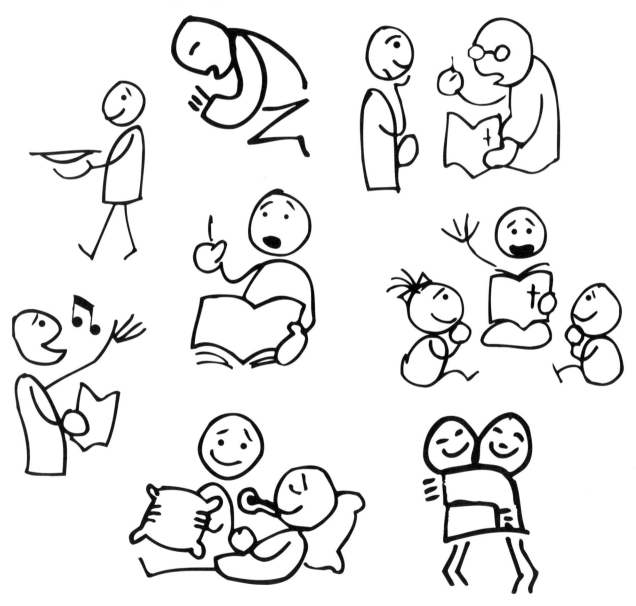

Preaching	Teaching the Bible
Teaching Children	Helping the Sick
Leading Singing	Praying
Serving Communion	Loving Each Other

God Is Great

Act It Out

Jesus taught the disciples that really loving people includes serving them. Jesus showed the disciples his love by doing all kinds of things to serve them.

Imagine...

Imagine that several of your friends have come over to spend time with you. How could you make the day special for them?

Act It Out!

Act out what you would do with your friends and be creative with different ways to make them feel special.

Props

stuffed animals for friends anything that you would need to show your friends your love

Answer Key

pg 33

Greet others warmly because Jesus would greet me warmly.

Do helpful things for people because Jesus helps me.

Say kind things to others because Jesus is kind to me.

Pray for others because Jesus prayed for me.

pg 36

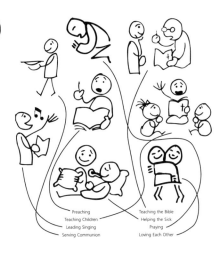

Preaching
Teaching Children
Leading Singing
Serving Communion

Teaching the Bible
Helping the Sick
Praying
Loving Each Other

pg 34

When there is a __problem__ ...

__talk__ about it right away!

__Get help__ if you need it.

Then __forgive__ and have a great day!

God Is Great

God's Great King

Parent

In Bible Class

Matthew 2, 6, 28; Mark 2, 3; Luke 2, 6

Your child will take an awesome journey back to the events surrounding Jesus' birth. She will learn ways God protected Jesus and his family, and she will relate to ways that God protects her now. Your child will learn that Jesus was worshiped as a king by the Magi then, but he is still the King of kings today. Ultimately, your child will be encouraged to consider how Jesus is Lord of his church—his kingdom—today!

Bringing It Home

In this chapter:

- Talk about life's worries; then talk about how God is able to take care of everything.
- Play a fun game about protection.
- Finish drawing the scene of Jesus' birthplace.
- Learn that Jesus asked us to go to all nations to teach others about God.
- Discover the names of the twelve apostles.
- Act out traveling to another country.

Just for Fun

- Look in a book or on the Web for a list of the wealthiest people in the world and how much they are worth. Try to help your child understand in general terms what this represents. For example: "Mr. Rich could probably buy a house as big as your school, Susie. And he probably could have his own swimming pool and basketball court...not to mention his own private airplane!" Help your child to understand that Jesus is "richer" and more powerful than all these people put together!
- Give your child a large piece of paper and coloring tools. Explain to her that the Bible teaches that angels watch over us and are commanded by God to help us. Ask your child to draw a big picture of the angel that watches over your family.
- Talk to your child about how God is God to people all over the world. Learn how to say "God is Great!" in several languages and teach your child these phrases. (There are probably disciples from many different countries in your congregation that can help you with this!)

God Is Great

Pages

Don't Worry

Matthew 6:31-33

Read this passage to your child and explain that Jesus was speaking to a large crowd that was gathered on the side of a mountain. Try to imagine how the people felt who were listening to Jesus.

Questions:
- What things do you worry about most?
- How do you feel when someone tells you not to worry about them?
- How does it make you feel to know that God knows what you need even before you do? Give some examples of this.

Bring It to Life!

Together with your child, make a list of things that you are most likely to worry about. Then open your Bible to Matthew 6:31-33 and ask: "Does God know that you are worried about _____? Do you think that God can take care of _____? How do you think that God wants you to feel about _____?"

Bring It to God!

Pray about each of the situations discussed above and thank God for the ways that he is working in your family.

Family Times

All Nations

Matthew 28:18-20

Read this passage to your child. Explain the concept of "authority" and then talk about how the disciples might have felt when Jesus said to go into "all nations"—especially since they did not have any modern forms of transportation at that time.

Questions:
- What does it mean that Jesus has "all authority in heaven and on earth"?
- If Jesus tells us to do something, we should do it. What are some things that Jesus told his disciples to do in these verses?
- Who do you know that has gone to a different nation to help make disciples?

Bring It to Life!

Talk with your child about different nations where there are churches. Help her to understand that the church is all over the world—not just in your city. Introduce your child to disciples who have served in nations other than your own. Make sure that your child understands that a disciple can make disciples anywhere—because "all nations" include the one you live in too! Encourage your child to get involved in Special Missions fundraising as a way of helping fulfill Jesus' great commission.

Bring It to God!

Pray as a family to make disciples of all nations right in your own neighborhood.

Brain Food

Have fun playing these games to learn and memorize feature scriptures.

No Trouble

You will protect me from trouble.
Psalm 32:7

What You'll Need
- sunblock
- bandages
- plastic gloves
- goggles
- Bible

Say the verse together several times. Hold up the different items and talk about how each one protects you in some way. Point out that God can protect us from trouble if we are trying to obey and follow his ways. Take one item, the sunblock for example, and say: "Sunblock, you will protect me from the sun, but God, you will protect me from trouble. Psalm 32:7." Do this with each item. Add other items to this activity. End by holding up your Bible and saying the verse from memory.

Good News for Everyone

[Jesus] said to them, "Go into all the world. Preach the good news to everyone."
Mark 16:15 (NIRV)

What You'll Need
- telephone book (residential white pages)

Say the verse together several times. Explain that these were Jesus' words to his disciples before he ascended (went back up) to heaven. Take out the telephone book and open it randomly. Close your eyes and point to any place on the page. Say the verse together and then ask, "To _____?" filling the blank with the name you pointed to. Lead the response by saying "Yes, to _____!" Have your child choose the next person to "pick and point" in the phone book. Continue until everyone has had a chance and you can say the verse from memory.

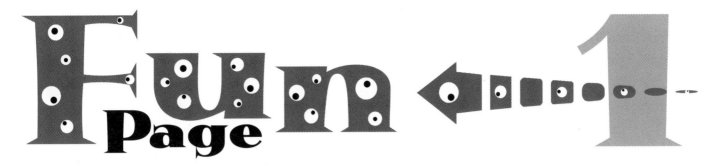

Instructions

Finish the picture below by drawing your own images of where Jesus was born. Don't forget to include any animals or people who came to visit him.

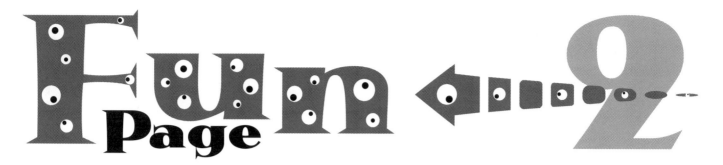

Instructions

Follow the dot-to-dot to see how God helped Mary and Joseph and baby Jesus. Follow the color code to color in the picture. Write the missing word in the blank.

God sent an _____ to protect Jesus. (Matthew 2:13)

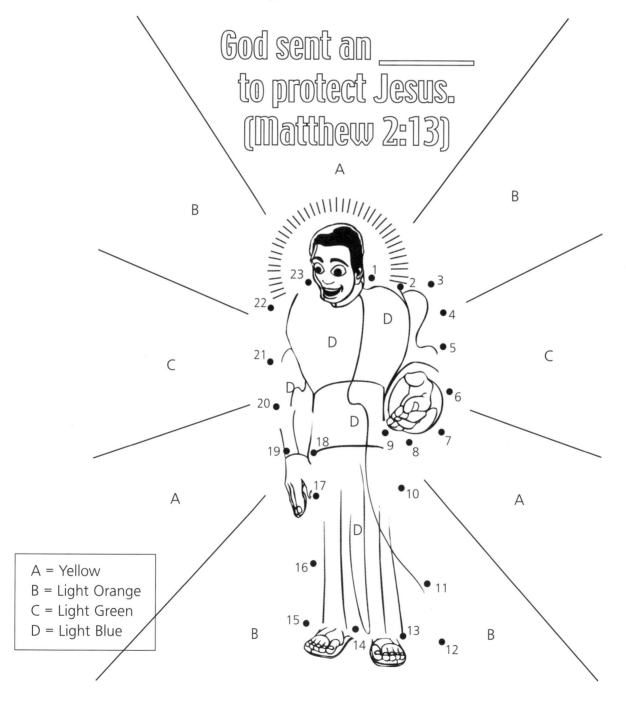

A = Yellow
B = Light Orange
C = Light Green
D = Light Blue

God Is Great

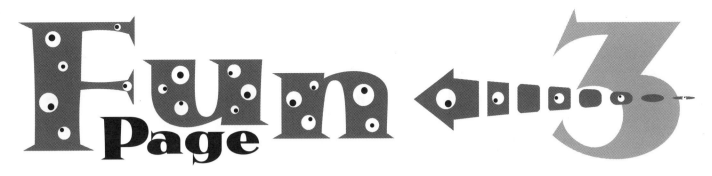

Fun Page 3

Circle the names of the twelve apostles that Jesus called to follow him. There are some false ones mixed in too, so be careful! You can look these up in the Bible in Mark 3:16-19.

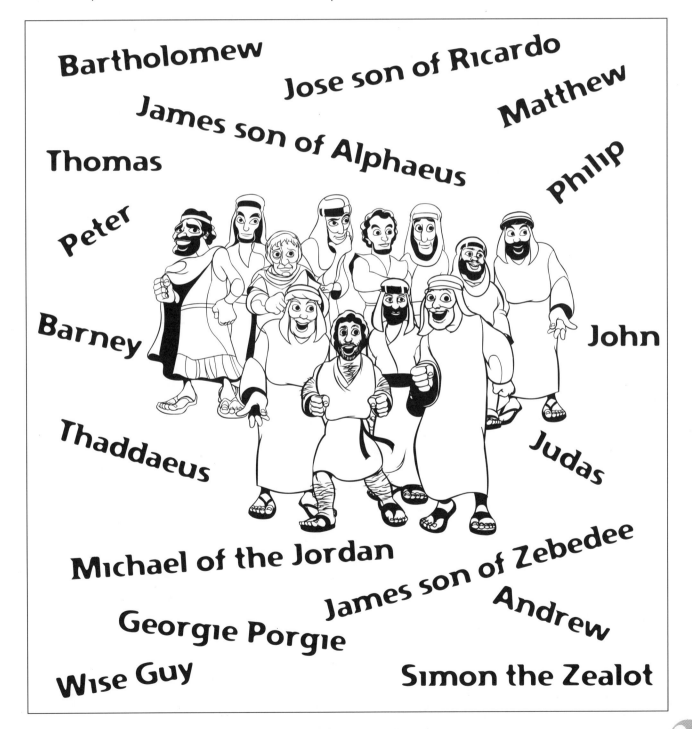

Bartholomew

Jose son of Ricardo

Matthew

James son of Alphaeus

Thomas

Philip

Peter

Barney

John

Thaddaeus

Judas

Michael of the Jordan

James son of Zebedee

Andrew

Georgie Porgie

Wise Guy

Simon the Zealot

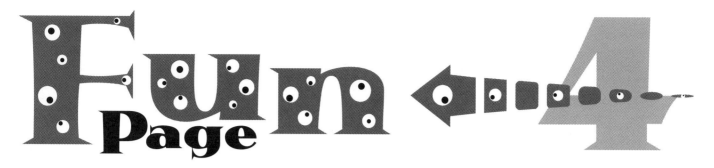

Instructions

Jesus teaches us not to worry because God will take of us, just as he takes care of the birds. In the picture below, how many birds can you find? Color them blue and draw a picture of yourself in the picture.

God Is Great

Act It Out

Jesus taught the disciples to go to all nations to make disciples. Some people travel to different countries to help others learn about God.

Imagine...

Imagine that you are asked to go with your family to a different country and help people learn about God.

Act It Out!

Act out how your parents would talk to you about this, how you would react and where you would go. What would you want to learn about before you went?

Props

suitcases
map
anything else for your voyage

Answer Key

pg 44 God sent an angel to protect baby Jesus.

pg 45 Peter, James son of Zebedee, John, Andrew, Philip, Bartholomew, Matthew, Thomas, James son of Alphaeus, Thaddaeus, Simon the Zealot, Judas

pg 46 There are 12 birds.

God Is Great

5

God's Great Champions

In Bible Class

Judges 4-7, Ezekiel 37, 1 Kings 18, Acts 10, 1 Samuel 17

God uses ordinary people to do extraordinary things for him. Using Gideon, Deborah, Ezekiel, Elijah, Cornelius and David, God led and protected his people. Your child will be amazed at how much God loves to encourage and strengthen the smallest and weakest among his people. Your child will be inspired to see how God can help him too.

Bringing It Home

In this chapter:
- Talk about Gideon overcoming his fear.
- Learn scriptures using a megaphone and binoculars.
- Count Gideon's soldiers.
- Discuss the story of Cornelius and Peter and how God wants everyone to know Jesus.
- Create front page news from Elijah's amazing victory stories.
- Act out a scene where lots of friends want to come to church.

Just for Fun

- Have a "smashing fears" evening with your family. Depending on the ages of your children, use balloons or building blocks for the following smashing time: Blow up the balloons and have everyone write on the balloons things or situations that make them afraid. Have fun popping and destroying those fears! If building blocks are preferred, build walls using the blocks, and then on the top of the wall tape pieces of paper with your fears written on them. Have fun smashing down the walls of fear!
- Invite for dinner a family from a different culture. Ask them to bring a dish that is representative of the food from their country to add to the meal you are preparing. Decorate the table in a way that will reflect some aspect of their culture. Ask your guests to share with your family some of the differences in their culture and yours.
- Create a special prayer night for your family. Light candles and pray for the leaders of your nation, your friends, church leaders, your child's teachers, etc. Make the time special and give everyone a chance to pray.

Pages

God Gets Gideon

Judges 6-7

Read the two chapters on Gideon and recount the story of this young warrior to your child. Read Judges 6:11-16 to your child. Talk about Gideon's fears and doubts. Then read Judges 7:13-18 to your child. Talk about how much God had helped Gideon to change.

Questions:

- Why was Gideon afraid to let God use him?
- What helped Gideon to overcome his fears and to trust God?
- What kinds of fears do you have?
- What are ways that God works to help you overcome your fears?

Bring It to Life!

Talk about how we need to remember the story of Gideon when we are afraid. Act out how to encourage a fearful person by recounting the story of Gideon in simple terms. Have fun "hamming up" the fearful side of Gideon.

Bring It to God!

Pray to have a heart that is willing to do what is right even when it is scary. Pray to see ways that God helps you to change.

Family Times

God Listens and Responds

Acts 10:1-8, 19-35, 47-48

Read the passages to your child or recount the story of Cornelius and Peter in your own words. Explain that this was an incredible account of God bringing very different people from different cities together to learn the story of Jesus.

Questions:

- What did God notice about Cornelius that caused Peter to be sent to him?
- Why do you think Cornelius had a lot of people with him when Peter came to visit?
- How did Peter feel about this situation?
- What did he do when he got to Cornelius's house?

Bring It to Life!

Share your own conversion story with your child. Talk about how God answered your prayers before and after your conversion. Ask your child to share about a prayer that he knows God answered.

Bring It to God!

Pray for people that you know you want to reach out to. Ask God to help you be like Peter and help someone who is interested in learning about Jesus.

Brain Food

Have fun playing these games to learn and memorize feature scriptures.

Call for Help

Then you will call, and the LORD will answer;
    you will cry for help, and he will say: Here am I.
Isaiah 58:9

What You'll Need
- cardboard tube or construction paper

Say the verse together several times. Talk about God's willingness to help us. All we need to do is ask! Using the cardboard tube as a "megaphone," take turns saying the verse to the family. (If you don't have a tube then curl the construction paper into a funnel, making a paper megaphone.) Encourage your child to say the verse boldly and confidently—knowing God will hear his call.

Prayer Partners

Spend a lot of time in prayer. Always be watchful and thankful.
Colossians 4:2 (NIRV)

What You'll Need
- binoculars (toy or real)

Say the verse together several times. Explain to your child that God wants us to pray a lot—but he also wants us to be thankful and watchful. Have each person in your family get a partner. Have one person say the first sentence while folding his hands in prayer. Then have his partner use the binoculars while saying the second sentence. Repeat and then switch roles until everyone can say both parts confidently.

God Is Great

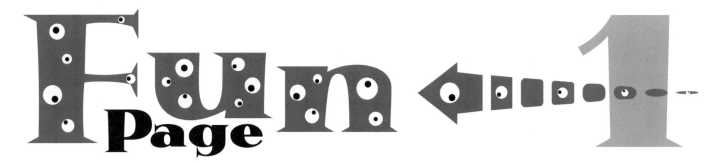

Fun Page 1

Look carefully at this scene of Gideon's men. Find the ten soldiers who are "standing and lapping water from their hands." Circle each one and number them from 1 to 10. Then fill in the blanks from the scripture with the words that are in the water.

Lord

mighty

warrior

with

When the angel of the Lord appeared to Gideon, he said,
"The _____ is _____ you, _____ _____ ."

Judges 6:12

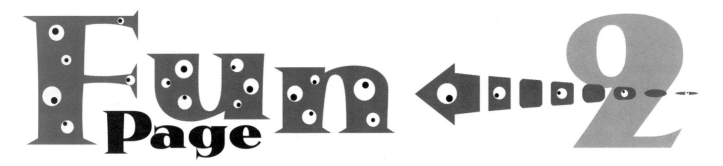

Instructions

Look at the picture of the soldier. Find the hidden letters that spell the name of the prophet who said that God could raise an army from dry bones.

_ _ _ _ _ _ _

God Is Great

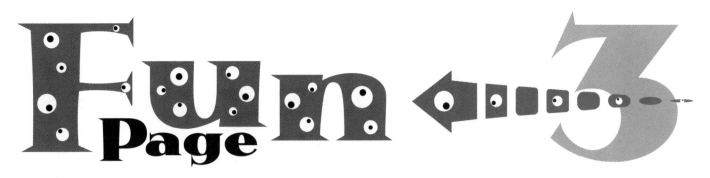

Instructions

Look at these four pictures on the left side. Read the headlines on the right that describe Elijah's amazing victory story. Draw a line from the picture to the headline it describes. Color the pictures.

"Elijah Soaks the Sacrifice!"

"Consuming Fire Proves that the Lord is God!"

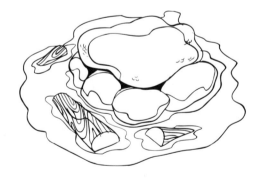

"King Ahab Accuses Elijah of Trouble Making!"

"Baal Prophets Sacrifice All Day—No One Responds"

God's Great Champions

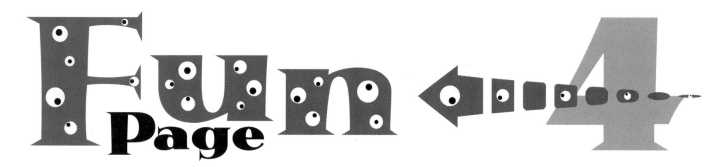

Instructions

Here is the scene where David defeats Goliath from 1 Samuel 17. Look for the words scattered on the stones in this picture. Find the words (from 1 Samuel 17:45) and use them to fill in the blanks.

"You come against _____ with _____ and _____ and _____, but I come against you in the name of the _____ ALMIGHTY."

spear

me

javelin

LORD

sword

Act It Out

In the story of Cornelius in Acts 10, the Bible says that God helped Peter to find Cornelius by showing him a vision and using other people to lead him. By the time Peter arrived at his house, there were many others there who also wanted to learn about Jesus. What an exciting surprise for Peter!

Imagine...

that your friend at school tells you that he wants to go to church with you. Imagine that when you arrive at his house to pick him up, he has five other friends or family members who want to come too!

Act It Out!

How would you feel?
What would you do?
How would you get everyone to church?

Props

telephone
large box for a car or bus

Answer Key

pg 53 "The Lord is with you, mighty warrior." (Judge 6:12)

pg 54 E Z E K I E L

pg 55

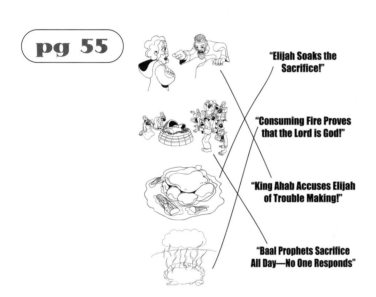

"Elijah Soaks the Sacrifice!"

"Consuming Fire Proves that the Lord is God!"

"King Ahab Accuses Elijah of Trouble Making!"

"Baal Prophets Sacrifice All Day—No One Responds"

pg 56 "You came against me with sword and spear and javelin, but I come against you in the name of the LORD ALMIGHTY." (1 Samuel 17:45)

God Is Great

God's Great Victory

In Bible Class

Matthew 4, 28; Mark 14-15; Luke 22; John 13

In this chapter, your child learns of Jesus' struggles with Satan. From his temptations in the desert, to his praying in the garden, to being betrayed by friends and then finally to his death on the cross, Jesus never gave in to sin. God brought a total victory over Satan by raising Jesus from the dead. Jesus' inspiring example of overcoming discouragement and fear will teach your child that she too can be victorious.

Bringing It Home

In this chapter:

- Talk about the heart and example of Jesus as he washed his disciples' feet.
- Learn scriptures while "following the leader."
- Unscramble the names of the twelve apostles.
- Discuss Jesus' loving and brave sacrifice on the cross.
- Solve a code that reveals God's love.
- Color a picture of Jesus' empty tomb.

Just for Fun

- Have a "man does not live on bread alone" dinner. Write out several encouraging scriptures that describe how we need to rely on God. Set the table and put scriptures at each place. Put a loaf of bread on the table and tell your family that you will be eating only bread for dinner. After you see their reaction, have each person read the scriptures in front of them and discuss how these words encourage all of you. Read Matthew 4:4 and then serve dinner. Thank God for the spiritual and physical food. Discuss how to imitate Jesus by reciting scriptures daily.
- Jesus died for the *whole* world. With your child, consider how many nations are represented in your local church. Write down all the different nationalities and languages that you know of and thank God that his word "works" in any language or nation.
- Have a "Garden of Gethsemane" experience with your child. Take your child to a special, quiet place to pray. Talk about how Jesus prayed in Gethsemane about things that were hard for him. Ask your child to pray for things that she is the most afraid of and/or things that are the most difficult for her. Let your child hear your prayers too—this will be a memorable time together.

Pages

Do As I Have Done for You

Mark 15:1-20, 33-37

Read these scriptures about Jesus' trial and death. Recount the story to your child in your own words. Explain that this was God's plan to send Jesus to earth to save us from our sins. (Focus on Jesus' response to all of this.)

Questions:
- Why do you think Jesus didn't fight or say anything during this time?
- Why do you think the other religious leaders did not like Jesus? Why did the soldiers make fun of him?
- How do you see God's love in this challenging situation?

Bring It to Life!
Have a discussion about what it means to honor someone who did something very heroic to save another person. If you could honor Jesus for saving you, what would you do? Write down your thoughts as a family and put this somewhere that you can see it to remind yourselves of your response.

Bring It to God!
Pray together to have the serving heart that Jesus expects of us. Pray that God will help you find specific ways to help people.

Family Times

Jesus on the Cross

Mark 15:1-20, 33-37

Read these scriptures about Jesus' trial and death. Recount the story to your child in your own words. Explain that this was God's plan to send Jesus to earth to save us from our sins. (Focus on Jesus' response to all of this.)

Questions:
- Why do you think Jesus didn't fight or say anything during this time?
- Why do you think the other religious leaders did not like Jesus? Why did the soldiers make fun of him?
- How do you see God's love in this challenging situation?

Bring It to Life!
Have a discussion about what it means to honor someone who did something very heroic to save another person. If you could honor Jesus for saving you, what would you do? Write down your thoughts as a family and put this somewhere that you can see it to remind yourselves of your response.

Bring It to God!
Thank God for Jesus' sacrifice and pray to remember to be grateful for it always.

Brain Food

Have fun playing these games to learn and memorize feature scriptures.

Bread and Bible

Jesus answered, "It is written: 'Man does not live on bread alone, but on every word that comes from the mouth of God.'"
Matthew 4:4

What You'll Need
- loaf of bread (in wrapper)
- Bible

Say the verse together several times. Sit in a circle with the family and pass the loaf of bread one direction and pass the Bible the other direction. While these are being passed have everyone say the verse together, ending with the reference. Whoever is holding the bread as the reference is said then says the first part of the verse alone. Whoever is holding the Bible says the second part of the verse. Repeat until everyone has had a chance to hold the bread and the Bible. Talk about how disciples need the Bible for spiritual survival. Help your child to understand that spiritually we all need "food" just like our bodies need the bread.

Follow the Leader

"I have set you an example that you should do as I have done for you."
John 13:15

What You'll Need
- props of your own choice

Say the verse together several times. Explain that this is Jesus speaking and he wanted the disciples to do things just like he did. Say the verse while doing something (e.g., clapping your hands, patting your head, tossing a pillow in the air, etc.). Have everyone repeat the verse after you while imitating the action you did. Let each person have a turn being the leader. Talk afterwards about how easy or difficult it was to lead or follow.

God Is Great

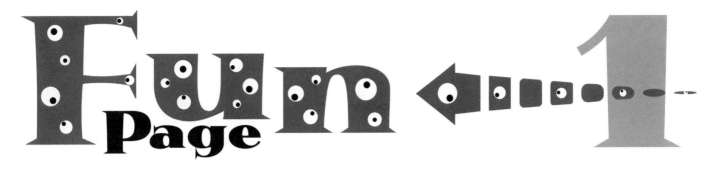

Fun Page 1

Instructions

Look at the box at the bottom of the page. Fill in the correct description or name next to the picture where it belongs.

_____

_____

_____

_____

_____

_____

angel	crowd and chief priests
servant of the high priest	Jesus
disciples and followers of Jesus	Judas the betrayer

God's Great Victory

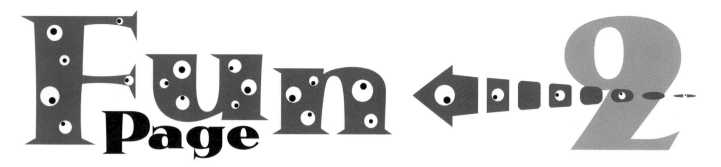

Fun Page 2

The Bible says that two women who had followed Jesus went to the tomb early on the third day to prepare Jesus' body. They were sad that Jesus had died—but they got a surprise when they arrived at the tomb! Color this picture using the color guide and your imagination.

1 = brown	5 = blue
2 = green	6 = gray
3 = tan	7 = yellow
4 = purple	

Instructions

In Matthew 28:2-7, an angel of the Lord came to Jesus' tomb and sat on the rock and talked to the women about Jesus. Finish drawing this scene of the angel at the tomb talking to the women.

Instructions

"Jesus loves the little children—all the children of the world!" How do we know that? Use the code below to find the answer in the verse.

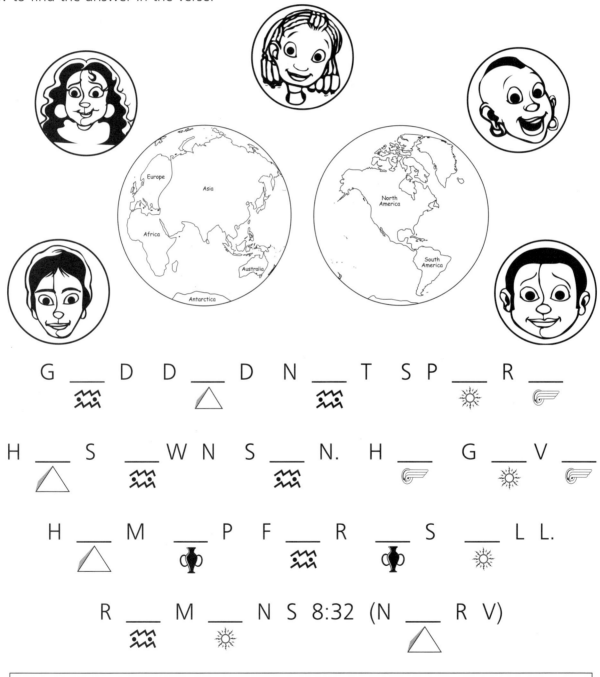

G _O_ D   D _I_ D   N _O_ T   SP _A_ R _E_

H _I_ S   _O_ WN   S _O_ N.   H _E_   G _A_ V _E_

H _I_ M   _U_ P   F _O_ R   _U_ S   _A_ LL.

R _O_ M _A_ N S 8:32 (N _I_ R V)

| A = ☀ | E = ✒ | I = △ | O = 〰 | U = ⚱ |

Act It Out

The Bible says that on the night before Jesus went to the cross, he went with his disciples to pray. When Jesus had finished praying, he found his friends fast asleep—they could not even stay awake to pray with him on this important night!

Imagine...

that you ask some friends to come over and keep you company the night before you are going to move far away. Imagine that they all fall asleep while you are trying to talk to them about how you are feeling.

Act It Out!

How would you feel?
What would you do?
What would you say to
your friends?

Props

suitcase
photo album
pillows

Answer Key

pg 63

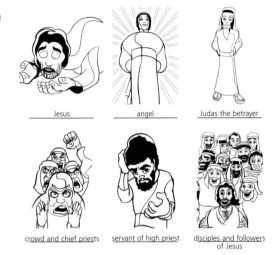

Jesus   angel   Judas the betrayer

crowd and chief priests   servant of high priest   disciples and followers of Jesus

pg 66 God did not spare his own Son. He gave him up for us all. Romans 8:32 (NIRV)

God Is Great

God's Great Missionaries

Parent

In Bible Class

Acts 1-2, 8; Philemon 1

Your child will learn about the amazing and powerful beginning of the church. The church experienced incredible victories and painful trials from the beginning, and your child will see how the disciples were determined to imitate Jesus. Paul's love for the church and the mission to bring the gospel to all the world is inspiring. Your child will see that God wants him to love the church and be a part of it too.

Bringing It Home

In this chapter:

- Talk about the exciting growth of the early church.
- Learn scriptures using candy and encouragement.
- Color and count the multiplying disciples.
- Discuss the importance of encouragement.
- Solve a maze by helping Philip teach and baptize the Ethiopian eunuch.
- Act out how to encourage a friend moving to a new country.

Just for Fun

- Find or borrow a church bulletin or video that describes the growth of the International Churches of Christ. Help your family to appreciate the ways the church is still multiplying today—around the world. Share with your child some personal experiences of people you've met who have become disciples.
- Encourage and refresh your family this week. Write on index cards specific things you appreciate about each person and put these cards in special places throughout the week. (e.g., in your child's lunch box, next to the toothbrush holder, on the mirror, in your husband's/wife's briefcase, etc.)
- Create a fun and simple scavenger hunt to help your family reach out to neighbors. For example, find a man in a red T-shirt and tell him about the neighborhood Bible Talk.

Pages

Miracle Grow

Acts 2:42-47, 4:4, 5:14

Read these passages to your child. Talk about how amazing it was for the church to grow so quickly. Explain that Jesus' death and resurrection were new ideas to these people.

Questions:

- Why was it important that the people devoted themselves to the apostles' teachings?
- Why you think they were so glad to hear the good news about Jesus?
- Does God want people to hear these things today? How can we tell them?

Bring It to Life!

Using dry cereal, small candies or pretzels, show how the church grew by multiplying. Explain that as each disciple shared his faith, people made the decision to repent and be baptized. Thus, one disciple becomes two, then four, then eight and so on. Show this by using the candies. Have fun watching the candies grow in number! A celebration may be in order—your child may want to eat up all that growth!

Bring It to God!

Thank God for the ways he worked in the early church to help the gospel spread. Pray for the same zeal to share about Jesus today.

Family Times

Joyful Refeshment

Philemon 1-7

Read this scripture and talk about what Paul felt for this disciple Philemon.

Questions:

- Would you have liked to know Philemon? Why?
- What does it mean to "be refreshing"?
- Why is it important to be loving to people, especially when we are sharing our faith with them?

Bring It to Life!

Have a Philemon encouragement craft time. Make several cards with hearts on them that say on the front "We love you because...." Then have your child write or dictate his feelings for a few of his friends or family members that he wants to encourage. After he gives them out or mails them, read Philemon 7 to him to encourage him for imitating Philemon.

Bring It to God!

Thank God for Philemon and Paul's friendship. Pray for God to help your family be very refreshing to others as well.

Brain Food

Have fun playing these games to learn and memorize feature scriptures.

All People

[God] wants everyone to be saved.
1 Timothy 2:4 (NIRV)

What You'll Need
- 7 Styrofoam cups
- bag of candy
- marker or pen

Say the verse together several times. Talk about how God gives everyone the opportunity to know him. Write on the outside of each cup one word from the verse (include the reference). Mix up the order of the cups and place them in a row on the table. Have the first person take a piece of candy and place it in the cup with the first word, "God." Then the next person puts a piece of candy in the cup with the second word, "wants." Continue all the way to the reference, and then have the person who puts the candy in the reference cup say the entire verse. Mix up the order of the cups and start over. Repeat until you run out of candy. Each person then gets a cup to save!

Refeshments

Your love has given me great joy and encouragement, because you, brother, have refreshed the hearts of the saints.
Philemon 7

What You'll Need
- no additional materials

Say the verse together several times. Talk about encouragement and refreshment, making sure everyone in your family knows what those words mean. Explain that there are many different ways to encourage others. Using the list below for ideas, pick a variety of ways for saying the verse while having fun encouraging one another!

Say the verse:
- while hugging one another
- in a whisper
- while snapping your fingers
- in a song or rap
- in a foreign accent
- while giving high-fives to each other

God Is Great

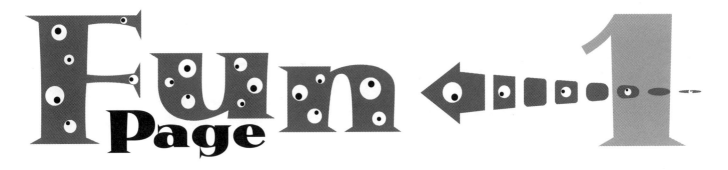

Fun Page 1

Instructions

In Acts 2, Peter preached to a large crowd! About three thousand people repented and were baptized that day. Can you count how many people are in the picture below? Color each face as you count it. Then, use your Bible to unscramble Acts 2:39 and write it correctly in the space provided.

"The children are far off and for your promise is for you and for all who—all will call the Lord our God whom."

_____

_____

_____

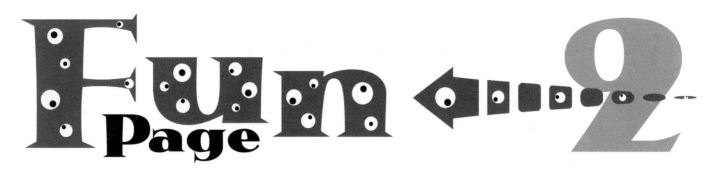

Instructions

In the book of Acts we learn that God added new people to the church every day! Do the math for each of the equations below. Then draw a line to the picture with the same number of people.

$1 + 1 =$ _____

$2 + 2 =$ _____

$4 + 4 =$ _____

$8 + 8 =$ _____

God Is Great

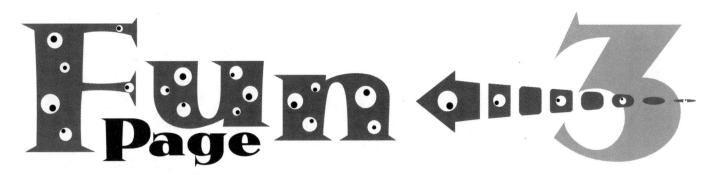

Instructions

The Ethiopian eunuch had a life-changing journey in Acts 8. Follow the pictures in the maze below and help Philip get to the Ethiopian so that he can teach and baptize him.

Start

Finish

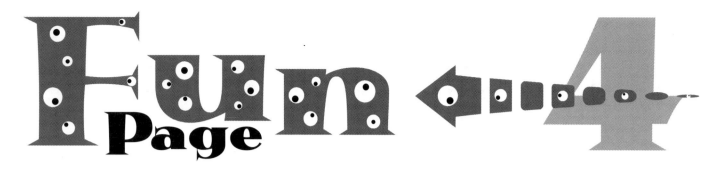

Fun Page 4

God sent Philip to help the Ethiopian eunuch learn about Jesus. Finish drawing the picture of Philip running to help the eunuch in his chariot.

Then Philip ran up to the chariot and heard
the man reading Isaiah the prophet.

Acts 8:30

God Is Great

Act It Out

In the early church, disciples often had to move to different places for their faith. Some people had to move because there was no church in their hometown. Others moved because of persecution against the church. Still others moved to help start new churches in places where there were no disciples.

Imagine...
that your best friend from church told you that his family was moving to a new country to help start a church there.

Act It Out!

How would you feel?
What would you say?
How could you encourage
your friend?

Props
world map
stationary or post cards
pictures

Answer Key

pg 73 There are 27 people. "The promise is for you and your children and for all who are far off—for all whom the Lord our God will call."

pg 75

God Is Great

God's Great Parables

Parent

In Bible Class

Matthew 13

The parables Jesus taught about God's kingdom will help your child see how amazing God's love and power are. Your child will learn that God has a great plan to see his kingdom grow and that this kingdom is truly life's greatest treasure.

Bringing It Home

In this chapter:

- Talk about the significance of the parables about God's kingdom.
- Learn scriptures while performing on stage and hunting for a treasure.
- Consider the treasures of the kingdom using a fun worksheet.
- Discuss the "treasures" of the kingdom.
- Hunt a "pearl of great value" in a special maze.
- Act out the discovery of an old, valuable treasure chest.

Just for Fun

- Have your family create some of your own parables. Using Jesus' parables as inspiration, try to come up with some modern-day stories that explain a spiritual truth. Have your family act them out together.
- Get a medium-size box with a lid, and have everyone help decorate it to look fancy like a treasure chest. Discuss all the ways God has blessed your family and how it's good to share these things with others. Have everyone contribute a gift to the treasure chest (nice toys they don't play with anymore or clothes they can share)—and go together to a children's home or hospital to give the gifts to those in need. Perhaps you can bring the box to encourage a family in your local church.
- If you have a girl in your family—have a jewelry making night. Bring beads and string, and make special bracelets and necklaces. Treasure the memories that times like this create. If you have enough supplies, make bracelets to give as gifts to your daughter's friends.

Pages

Make a Difference

Matthew 13:31-33

Read the scriptures to your child. Explain how the tiny mustard seed and the tiny bit of yeast can make a big difference. Talk about how God's church grows around the world to be a great presence and how Jesus' teachings can cause big changes in people's lives anywhere and at anytime.

Questions:
- Why do you think God wanted us to know that his kingdom is like a mustard seed? How can this give us hope?
- How can we be like yeast and make a difference in our world?
- Why is it encouraging to know that big things can happen from something so small?

Bring It to Life!
If possible, make two loaves of bread from scratch (or divide one loaf recipe in half). Omit the yeast in one of the loaves. Let your child see the difference after the loaves have had time to rise. Bake both and compare the differences in taste and consistency. Your child will have a greater understanding of how much difference the yeast makes. The same is true of God's kingdom.

Bring It to God!
Thank God for his wonderful parables that help us to understand spiritual things in an easier way. Pray for God's kingdom to grow powerfully around the world in our time.

Family Times

Hidden Treasure

Matthew 13:44

Ask your child to write down something that is very valuable to her. Ask her if she found a treasure chest full of something really awesome, what would it be? How would she feel after finding it? Read the scripture to her. Talk about how excited this man was and how he might have acted after he found it.

Questions:
- Why does this parable help us to feel happy about God's kingdom?
- Why do you think the man sold all he had to be able to have this treasure?
- How can we value God's kingdom as much as this man valued the treasure?

Bring It to Life!
Give each person in your family a piece of paper. Have each person draw a large treasure chest and then write inside of it all the ways that knowing God and his church is valuable to them personally. Have each person read their answers.

Bring It to God!
Thank God together for all the ways he makes your life "rich."

Brain Food

Have fun playing these games to learn and memorize feature scriptures.

Star Bright

Shine like stars in the universe as you hold out the word of life.
Philippians 2:15-16

What You'll Need
- microphone (or something to represent a microphone)
- stage or spotlight
- props as needed

Say the verse together several times. Talk about stars and their beauty in the dark sky. Explain that when we share the Bible with others, God thinks we shine like stars! Talk about famous "stars"—movie stars, rock stars or athletes. Encourage each family member to pick their favorite "star" and give them the microphone to say the verse as this person would say it (or sing it). Encourage them to use props if needed (e.g., say the verse as Michael Jordan while bouncing a basketball). Try to create a stage or spotlight for the person performing. Have fun and encourage everyone's attempts. When you are done, suggest they share the verse with a friend. That way they can be God's shining star!

Trick or Treat

"The kingdom of heaven is like treasure hidden in a field."
Matthew 13:44

What You'll Need
- small bag of candies or "treats"
- small bag of crumpled paper
- 3 Styrofoam cups

Say the verse together several times. Talk about treasures and treats. Explain that Jesus is teaching his disciples how valuable and precious the kingdom is—he compares it to a treasure! Turn the cups upside down and put the candies ("treat") under one cup, put the crumpled paper ("trick") under the next cup and put nothing under the third cup. Mix up the cups. Have your child say the verse from memory and then pick a cup. If it is the treat, then let her be the one to mix up the cups and pick the next person. If that person picks the trick, then have them say the verse again and start the process over again. If they pick the empty cup, have them say the verse. Start over and repeat until everyone gets a chance to pick the treat. At the end, open the bag of treats and share the "treasure" with everyone!

God Is Great

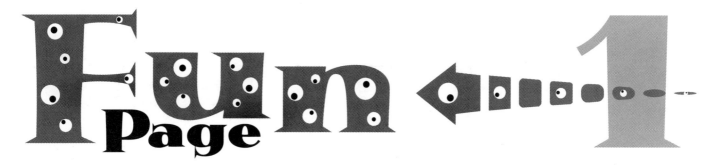

Fun Page

Instructions

Search for five "treasures" that God gives us in his kingdom today and write them in the spaces provided at the bottom of the page.

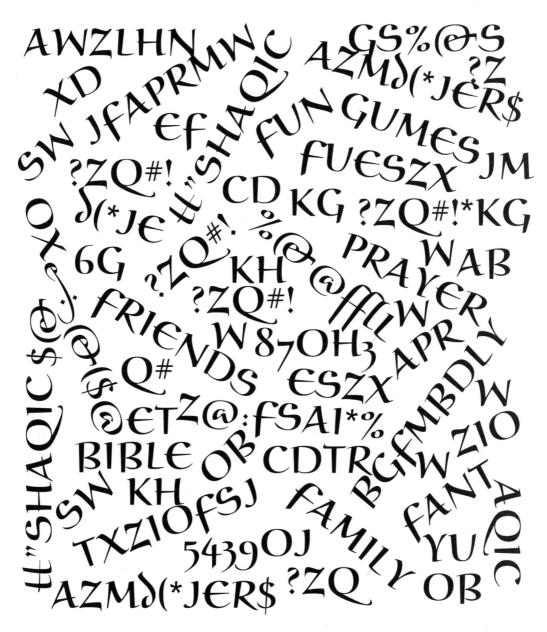

_____ _____

_____ _____

God's Great Parables

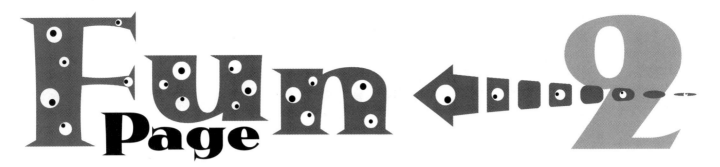

Fun Page 2

Instructions

Jesus explained that the kingdom of heaven was like a merchant who was searching for pearls. Help the merchant on this page to find the "pearl of great value."

Start

Finish

God Is Great

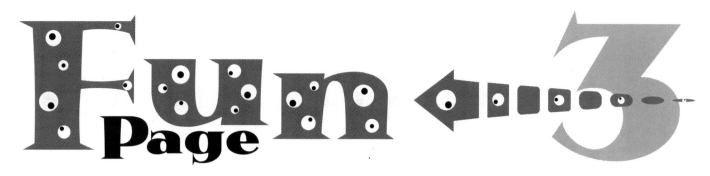

Fun Page 3

Instructions

Think about the different kingdom treasures that you have been learning about. Look at the different treasures on this page, and color the ones that are true "kingdom treasures"—ones that you can't buy in a store but can only come from God.

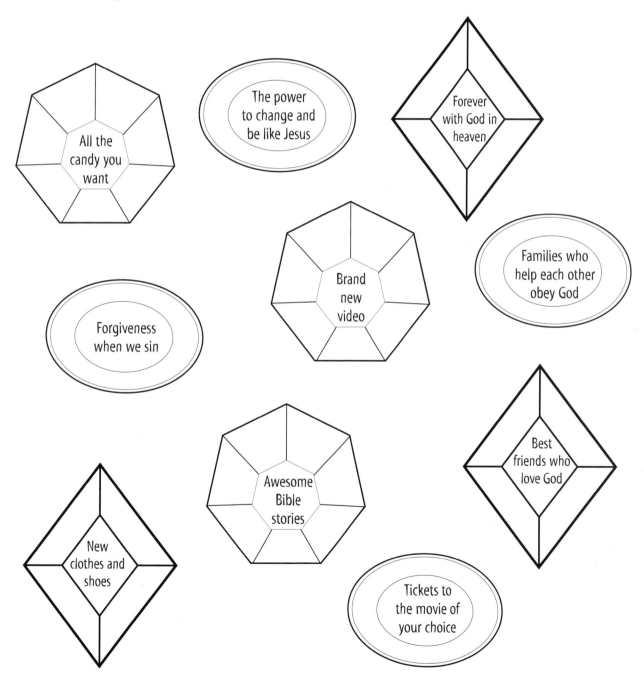

All the candy you want

The power to change and be like Jesus

Forever with God in heaven

Forgiveness when we sin

Brand new video

Families who help each other obey God

New clothes and shoes

Awesome Bible stories

Best friends who love God

Tickets to the movie of your choice

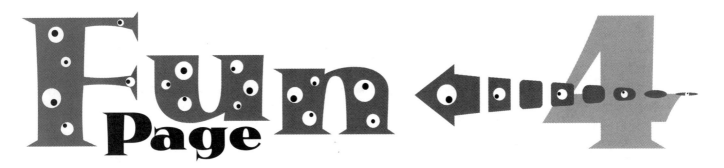

Instructions

Use your Bible to look up the parables in Matthew 13. Then draw a line matching each reference to the parable it best describes. Color the pictures.

Parable of the
mustard seed

Matthew 13:33

Matthew 13:44

Parable of the
hidden treasure

Matthew 13:45-46

Parable of the yeast

Matthew 13:31-32

Parable of the pearl
of great value

God Is Great

Act It Out

The Bible teaches us that Jesus used stories called "parables" to teach people about God and heaven. Jesus told many parables because it helped the people understand important ideas about obeying God and loving others. Several of Jesus' parables described the kingdom of God as something precious and valuable.

Imagine...

that you were outside in your backyard digging a hole. Imagine that your shovel hit something hard. You dig further and uncover an old chest—a treasure chest!

Act It Out!

What would you do?
Who would you tell?

Props

small shovel or garden trowel
old chest

Answer Key

pg 83   fun, friends, prayer, Bible, family

pg 84

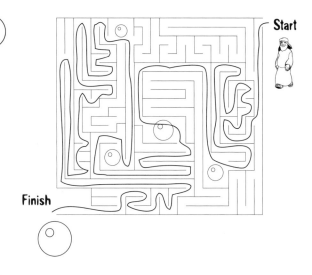

pg 85

  – Best friends who love God
  – Awesome Bible stories
  – Forever with God in heaven
  – The power to change and be like Jesus
  – Families who help each other obey God
  – Forgiveness when we sin

pg 86

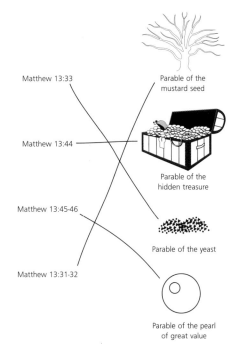

Matthew 13:33   Parable of the mustard seed

Matthew 13:44   Parable of the hidden treasure

Matthew 13:45-46   Parable of the yeast

Matthew 13:31-32   Parable of the pearl of great value

God Is Great

9

God's Great Miracles

Parent

In Bible Class

John 2, 20; Matthew 14; Luke 8

There are many awe-inspiring miracles that Jesus performed to help the people see God's power up close. Your child will be impressed by the variety of Jesus' miracles and will see that Jesus is worthy of our faith in him. It is even more inspiring to believe that his power is still at work today.

Bringing It Home

In this chapter:

- Talk about Jesus and Peter walking on water.
- Learn scriptures with energetic and eye-opening games.
- Finish pictures while discovering truths about several of Jesus' miracles.
- Discuss how it might feel to be healed by Jesus.
- Unscramble Jesus' miracles.
- Act out being in a boat while Jesus calms a raging storm.

Just for Fun

- Help your child to appreciate the work of fishermen and the power of the weather. Go to the library and check out books about both of these topics. If there is a nautical museum in your area, take the family for a visit. Read Mark 4:35-41 together and discuss as a family the magnitude of this "squall" (seasoned fishermen were afraid!) and the magnitude of Jesus' power to calm it.
- As a family, make a "faith" list. Have everyone share something they need faith to face, overcome, do or become in the upcoming week. Write these things on a poster and put it where everyone can see it during the week. Pray for each situation—in faith. Share victory stories the following week.
- The disciples worshiped Jesus after he performed a miracle. Talk to your family about worship and what it means. Look up several scriptures and prepare a worship time. Suggestions: light candles, sing worshipful songs, share things you are thankful for, pray, invite another family to join you.

God Is Great

Pages

On the Water

Matthew 14:22-33

Read the passage to your child. Talk about how scary it could have been to be on that boat at night. Discuss how courageous Peter was in the midst of a scary time. Ask your child who are some people that he thinks "walk on water" (step out on faith).

Questions:

- Why is what Peter did an amazing show of faith? Why is Jesus so amazing here?
- Why did Peter start to sink?
- How can we be like Peter and sometimes doubt and be afraid?

Bring It to Life!

Have a "fix your eyes on Jesus" devotional time. List all the miracles that you can think of that Jesus did. Pick out several songs about Jesus and sing them. Talk about all the ways that Jesus helped people to overcome their doubts. Have each person share what they love most about Jesus.

Bring It to God!

Pray that God will help you to remember Jesus and to keep "fixed" on him when times are scary or difficult.

Family Times

Healing a Paralyzed Man

Mark 2:1-12

Read the passage to your child. Talk about what a paralytic is: a big word that means "paralyzed." He could not feel or move his legs. He was helpless to go to Jesus himself. But he had friends who helped him.

Questions:

- How do you think this man felt when his friends were lowering him through a hole in the roof to see Jesus?
- Since the roof was made of dirt and straw, what do you think was happening when they started digging the hole for their friend?
- Why do you think his friends were willing to go to so much trouble to get him to Jesus?
- How can we also bring people to Jesus?

Bring It to Life!

Ask your child, "Do you remember seeing people in wheelchairs?" Tell your child that often they are in wheelchairs because their legs are paralyzed; they cannot feel them, and they cannot walk. Sometimes they cannot move other parts of their bodies, like their arms or hands. Take turns sitting in a chair and playing like you cannot move your legs or your arms. Have each person tell how it makes them feel not to be able to move and how it would feel if Jesus were to heal them.

Bring It to God!

Ask your child to think of someone you know who is paralyzed or very sick. Then pray that God will help the person in ways that are best for him.

Brain Food

Have fun playing these games to learn and memorize feature scriptures.

Faith and Deeds

Show me your faith without deeds, and I will show you my faith by what I do.
James 2:18

What You'll Need
• no additional materials

Say the verse together several times. Talk about faith and deeds. Explain the importance of faith and deeds working together. Say the verse together as a family. When you get to the word "faith" have everyone stand up tall. When you get to the word "deeds" have everyone kneel down and pat the floor. Keep saying the verse faster and faster, until you are popping up and down, up and down and everyone needs a breath!

Go God!

"What is impossible with men is possible with God."
Luke 18:27

What You'll Need
• pictures of nature (mountains, sky, animals, volcano, etc.)

Say the verse together several times. Show your family the pictures you selected. Talk about God's power to create and control these things. Then ask questions (as suggested below) taking turns answering with the memory verse. For example: "Can Mommy make mountains?" The answer would be, "No. What is impossible with men is possible with God, Luke 18:27." Repeat until everyone can say the verse from memory. Talk about anything your child feels concerned or anxious about this week. Remind him that anything is possible with God.

Suggested questions:
Can you paint the sky?
Can Daddy stop (or start) a volcano?
Can Susie bring peace to the nations?
Did Johnny give the zebra its stripes?

God Is Great

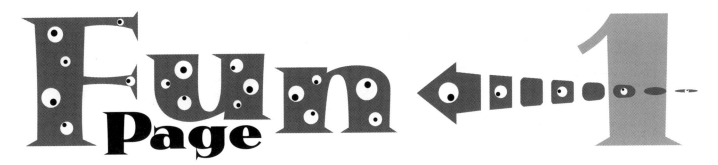

Instructions

Jesus did his first miracle at a wedding in Cana (John 2:1-11). Read the phrases on the left side of the page, and then draw a line to the picture that it best describes on the right side of the page. When you are finished, write the story in your own words at the bottom.

Jesus and Mary at the wedding.

Mary notices that the wine has run out.

Jesus turns water to wine.

People are happy at the wedding.

_____

_____

_____

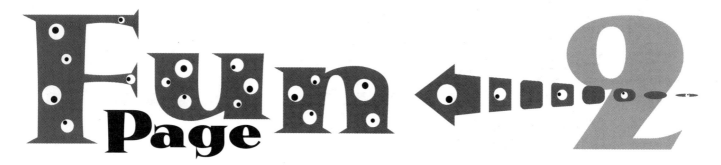

Fun Page 2

The disciples got a big surprise the night that they saw Jesus walk on the water. Finish drawing this picture of the boat, and then answer the question below. Use the letters hiding in the net to help you figure out the answer to this question. Hint: Use your Bible to find the answer in Matthew 14:33.

Do you know what the disciples did after they saw Jesus walk on the water?

— — — — — — — — — — —

God Is Great

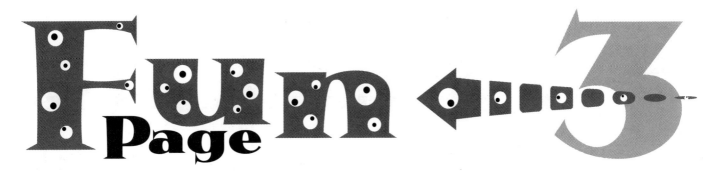

Instructions

When Jesus calmed the storm, the disciples were amazed! Look at these two pictures and then write the words from the box next to the picture they best describe. Before coloring the pictures, think about the different colors you will use. What color is a stormy sky? What color is a peaceful sky? What color is a stormy sea? What color is a calm sea?

| Fear |
| Calm |
| Worry |
| Peace |
| Upset |
| Amazed |

_____

_____

_____

_____

_____

_____

God's Great Miracles

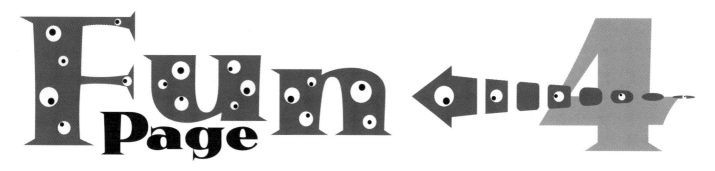

Fun Page 4

Instructions

Jesus did amazing miracles! The phrases below are a little mixed-up. Can you write the correct words in the phrases at the bottom of the page?

"Changing Water into a Storm?"

"Calming a Paralyzed Man?"

"Walking on Wine?"

"Healing Water?"

"Changing Water into _____"

"Calming a _____"

"Walking on _____"

"Healing _____"

God Is Great

Act It Out

Over and over again, Jesus showed that he had power to do amazing things—from healing the blind to raising the dead. What is more, Jesus proved that he was the supreme "weather man" because he had God's power over the wind and the ocean. Each time that Jesus did a miracle, he proved that he had God's power, and more people put their faith in him.

Imagine...

that you were on the same boat as Jesus and the disciples when a great storm arose. Imagine listening to the twelve disciples crying for helping and fearing for their lives. Imagine that you see Jesus wake up and calm the storm entirely.

Act It Out!

What would you say?
What would you do?
What would you think about Jesus' power?

Props

bucket
toy boat and water
life jacket

Answer Key

pg 93

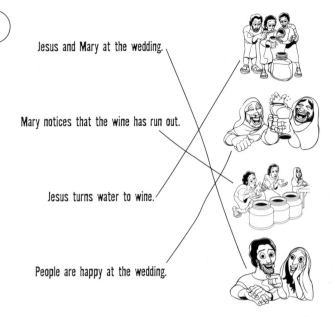

Jesus and Mary at the wedding.

Mary notices that the wine has run out.

Jesus turns water to wine.

People are happy at the wedding.

pg 94   worshiped

pg 96
– Changing Water into Wine
– Calming a Storm
– Walking on Water
– Healing a Paralyzed Man

God's Great Gift of Choice

In Bible Class

Luke 2, 10; 1 Samuel 15, 20; Acts 9, 16; Daniel 1

Good company builds good character. Your child will examine the character of several men and women as they consider godly and ungodly characteristics. As she witnesses several godly characters to imitate, she will be warned to avoid the ungodly character traits such as King Saul's disobedience and Martha's anxiety.

Bringing It Home

In this chapter:

- Talk about Jesus at the temple when he was a young boy.
- Learn scriptures while playing a variation of the game "Duck, Duck, Goose."
- Find hidden words that explain Daniel's motivation.
- Learn about the dangers of jealousy in a friendship.
- Write headlines for David and Jonathan's special friendship.
- Act out a hero from the Bible.

Just for Fun

- Have a "Bible Jeopardy" game night. Invite another family to join the fun. Create questions and answers from the Bible stories your family has been reading. Categorize the questions by age, so everyone can compete with someone on their age level. Make it fun and creative. Perhaps have prizes for the winners.
- Help your child plan a "David and Jonathan" day. Talk about David and Jonathan's special friendship, then have your child invite her best friend over for the day. Help your child plan a day of fun and spiritual bonding activities. This can help your child build a friendship for life!

Pages

Jesus at the Temple

Luke 2:41-52

Read this passage to your child and explain that as a young boy, Jesus wanted to be pleasing to God. He could have been playing with the kids on the way back to Nazareth, but instead, he was at the temple asking questions about God and listening to the answers given by the leaders.

Questions:
- Why do you think Jesus stayed at the temple?
- Why were the people amazed at Jesus?
- Who can you ask questions about God?
- What kind of questions would you like to ask?

Bring It to Life!
Ask your child to think of a twelve-year-old boy she knows. What kinds of things does he like to do? Look through magazines together and cut out pictures of things the boy likes to do. Paste these pictures around the edges of a piece of paper. Then on the inside of the paper, have your child draw a picture of this boy learning about God. Talk with your child about this being the center and most important part of his life.

Bring It to God!
Pray with your child about specific people you and your family can teach about God.

Family Times

Friends Forever

1 Samuel 20

Read parts of the story to your child and explain the more difficult parts. Emphasize the fact that even though Jonathan knew that David was eventually going to become the king instead of him, he still loved David and was his best friend.

Questions:
- Who was Saul's son?
- Usually the king's son becomes king when his father dies. Why was David going to become king instead of Jonathan?

- Why might Jonathan be jealous of David? But was he? (no)
- When might you be jealous? Have there been times when someone got to do something you wanted to do? How did you feel?

Bring It to Life!
Come up with several scenarios from school, home and Bible class in which someone is picked to do something or to have a certain role. In each scenario, act out with your child the way she would respond if she were jealous. Then have her act out being happy for the person who was chosen.

Bring It to God!
Pray with your child, asking God to help her love her friends and to be happy when good things happen to them.

Brain Food

Have fun playing these games to learn and memorize feature scriptures.

Hold It

If your tongue tells lies, you will get into trouble.
Proverbs 17:20 (NIRV)

What You'll Need
• no additional materials

Say the verse together several times. Talk about the dangers of lying and how harmful it is. Explain that telling the truth makes everything clear and easy to understand. Take turns saying the verse while holding your tongue. (Obviously it will be silly and difficult to understand!) Then say the verse normally—and it will be clear and easy to understand. Do this until your child knows the verse. If necessary, use this opportunity to address any "issues" around the home—either praising your child for telling the truth or challenging her for lying.

NOTE: Make sure everyone washes their hands before and after this game!

The Helper

There was a disciple named Tabitha who was always doing good and helping the poor.
Acts 9:36

What You'll Need
• doll or picture of a woman (to represent Tabitha)

Say the verse together several times. Sit in a circle with your family and talk about Tabitha and how the Bible mentions her helping the poor. Play this variation of "Duck, Duck, Goose." Choose one person to be Tabitha. Have her walk around the outside of the circle saying the memory verse. The people in the circle can help her if she can't remember all the words. When "Tabitha" says the reference she drops the doll behind someone and tags them. That person then becomes the new "Tabitha" and they switch places. Repeat the process until everyone has had a chance to be Tabitha. End the time by discussing ways your family can help the poor.

God Is Great

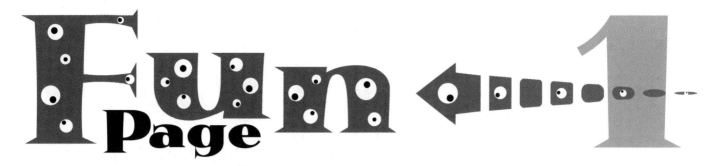

Fun Page 1

Instructions

The Bible tells us that Jesus loved to be in his father's house. That means that he loved to worship God and he loved to be around others who worshiped God too. The teachers who heard him were amazed at his ability to answer their questions. If you could ask Jesus some questions, what would they be? Write them in the box on this page and then draw a picture of a group of people around Jesus on the steps of the temple.

Everyone who heard him was amazed at his understanding and his answers.
Luke 2:47

God's Great Gift of Choice

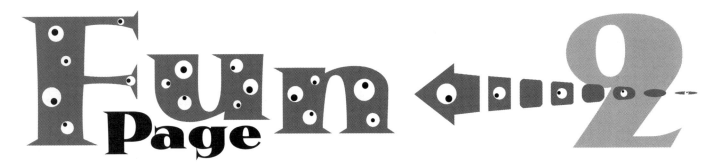

Fun Page 2

Instructions

Daniel and his friends were very serious about pleasing God—even if it got them in trouble. Use the words hidden in this picture to answer the question below: If you asked Daniel and his friends why they ate only vegetables, what would they say? (Hint: look up the answer in 1 Thessalonians 2:4b.)

_____

_____

God Is Great

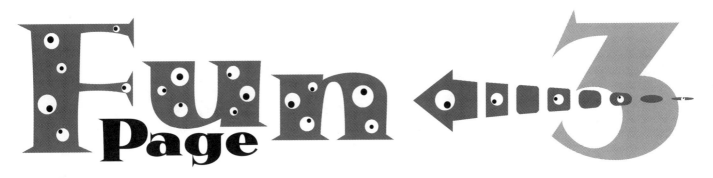

Instructions

David and Jonathan had a friendship that showed their love for God and each other. Look at the four pictures and draw a line to the headline that best describes each one.

David and Jonathan make a plan and a promise.
King Saul is angry at David.
Jonathan risks his life to save David.
Jonathan and David pledge friendship forever.

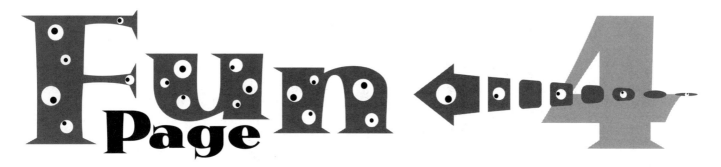

Instructions

Look at the statements below that describe the men and women you have been learning about. Find the missing word and write it in the space where it belongs.

Jesus : He loved to spend time at the _____.

Mary : She focused on _____ to Jesus.

Martha : She was _____ and anxious about many things.

Saul : He disobeyed and did not tell the _____.

David and : They were _____ forever!
Jonathan

Tabitha : She was always _____ the poor.

Lydia : She was eager and grateful to be a _____.

DANIEL : HE PLEASED _____, NOT MEN.

disciple	truth
helping	listening
worried	temple
friends	God

God Is Great

Act It Out

The Bible gives us many examples of men and women who loved God and chose to live their lives God's way. It also tells us what happened to those people who did not. God wants us to live every day in a way that shows other people the truth about Jesus.

Imagine...

that you could choose to be just like one of the people in the Bible from this chapter. Who would you choose to be like? Jesus? Mary? David or Jonathan? Tabitha? Lydia? Daniel?

Act It Out!

What would you do? What would you say?

Props

robes for Bible-time costumes

Answer Key

pg 104 We are not trying to please men but God.

pg 105

pg 106

Jesus : He loved to spend time at the __temple__ .

Mary : She focused on __listening__ to Jesus.

Martha : She was __worried__ and anxious about many things.

Saul : He disobeyed and did not tell the __truth__ .

David and : They were __friends__ forever!
Jonathan

Tabitha : She was always __helping__ the poor.

Lydia : She was eager and grateful to be a __disciple__ .

Daniel : He pleased __God__ , not men.

God Is Great

Year Two
Curriculum Overview

Unit	Lesson	Lesson Text	Focus	Life Application	Scripture Memory Verse
FALL 1 12. The Bible	1. God Gave Us the Bible	2 Timothy 3:16-17 Psalm 46:10	• The Bible helps us to know God.	God wants to talk to us today through the Bible.	2 Timothy 3:16
	2. The Old Testament	Hebrews 1:1 Romans 15:4	• God spoke through the prophets.	God is trying to get people to listen to him.	Hebrews 1:1 (ICV)
	3. The New Testament	John 14:26 John 15:26 John 20:30-31	• The New Testament helps us to be like Jesus.	God wants us to remember his words.	John 14:26 (ICV)
	4. Putting It All Together	Ephesians 2:20-22	• The Bible is the foundation of the church today	God wants us to make the Bible the foundation for our lives today	Matthew 7:24 (ICV)
13. What is a Disciple?	1. Putting God First	Luke 5:1-9 Luke 9:23-24	• A disciple obeys God no matter what.	God wants me to obey, no matter what.	Luke 5:5
	2. Depending On God	Luke 11:1-13	• God wants to give us everything we need.	God wants me to pray everyday.	Luke 11:9 (NIRV)
	3. Make That Change	Luke 15:11-24	• A disciple is willing to change.	God wants me to change when I do wrong.	Matthew 18:3
	4. Putting It All Together	John 3:1-8 Acts 2:38	• A true disciple has a new birth.	All kinds of people are born again.	John 3:3
14. The Church	1. Best Friends	John 13:34-35	• Best friends in church	God wants our friends to love God like we do.	John 13:35 (NIRV)
	2. Resolving Conflict	Matthew 5:23-24 Matthew 18:15-16	• Resolving conflict	We can't love God if we don't love each other.	John 13:34 (ICV)
	3. Leaders	Hebrews 13:7, 17	• Knowing and respecting leaders	God gives us people in the church who help us do the right thing.	Hebrews 13:7
	4. The Body	1 Corinthians 12:12-27	• Concept of the body	Every person is important to God's church.	1 Corinthians 12:27
15. King of Kings	1. The King Is Born	Luke 2:1-20	• God gives and protects.	God gave us Jesus to lead and protect us.	Luke 2:11
	2. The King Is Protected	Matthew 2:1-18	• God takes care of me.	God can do amazing things to protect us.	Psalm 32:7
	3. The King Has Servants	Mark 3:13-19	• God has a purpose for my life.	Jesus still wants people to do his work.	Mark 3:14 (ICV)
	4. The Kingdom Comes First	Matthew 6:25-34	• God takes care of us. • His purpose comes first.	We shouldn't worry. God knows what we need.	Matthew 6:33 (NIRV)
	5. The Kingdom Is for All	Mark 16:15	• Jesus loves everybody.	God wants all people to be in his church.	Mark 16:15 (NIRV)
	6. The Kingdom Today	Matthew 28:16-20	• World Missions	God's kingdom is growing today.	Matthew 28:19

Year Two Curriculum Overview

Unit	Lesson	Lesson Text	Focus	Life Application	Scripture Memory Verse
16. God's Awesome Victories	1. Gideon	Judges 6-7	• God has a plan for our lives.	God can use anybody who is willing to do his work.	Judges 6:14
	2. Deborah	Judges 4-5	• God takes care of me.	God provides leaders to help us.	Isaiah 58:9
	3. Ezekiel	Ezekiel 37:1-14	• God is father.	God wants people to be full of his spirit.	Ezekiel 37:14
	4. Elijah	1 Kings 18:16-46	• God takes care of me.	God wants people to know that he is God.	1 Kings 18:36
	5. Cornelius	Acts 10	• prayer	God is looking for people who want to know him.	Colossians 4:2
	6. David and Goliath	1 Samuel 17:31-50	• God takes care of me.	God wants me to be victorious.	1 Samuel 17:45
17. Jesus Defeats Satan	1. Jesus Is Tempted	Matthew 4:1-11	• Jesus depended on God.	We need to rely on God's word.	Matthew 4:4
	2. The Last Supper	John 13:1-17	• Serving	We need to serve like Jesus served.	John 13:15
	3. Jesus' Friends Leave	Mark 14:43-50, 66-72; Luke 22:39-53	• self-denial; prayer	God can help me with self-control.	Luke 22:42 (NIRV)
	4. The Cross	Mark 15:1-40	• self-denial • Jesus died for all	God wants to love all people like Jesus did.	Romans 8:32 (NIRV)
	5. He's Alive!	Matthew 28:1-10	• God raised Jesus from the dead.	God can change the most difficult situation.	Matthew 28:6
	6. Jesus Says "Go!"	Matthew 28:16-20	• Jesus' purpose	We need to go and tell.	John 20:21
18. Early Church and Missions	1. Pentecost	Acts 1-2	• God keeps his promises. • God is powerful.	The church is the kingdom on earth today.	Acts 2:39
	2. The Church Grows	Acts 2:47, 4:4, 5:14	• Jesus loves all people.	Jesus still wants all people to know him today.	1 Timothy 2:4 (NIRV)
	3. The Early Church	Philemon 1:1-7	• Best friends in the church	We can go with our friends to tell others about God.	Philemon 7
	4. The Ethiopian Eunuch	Acts 8:26-40	• God has a plan for our lives.	God is always helping people to find him.	Acts 8:30-31
19. Parables	1. The Mustard Seed	Matthew 13:31-32	• God is powerful.	God wants the church to grow.	Matthew 13:34
	2. Yeast	Matthew 13:33	• The church grows.	How do I influence other people?	Philippians 2:15-16
	3. Hidden Treasure	Matthew 13:44	• God is always good.	God is the most valuable treasure.	Matthew 13:44
	4. Pearl	Matthew 13:45-46	• God is always good.	We must look to find God's treasure.	Matthew 13:45

Year Two
Curriculum Overview

Unit	Lesson	Lesson Text	Focus	Life Application	Scripture Memory Verse
20. Jesus' Miracles	1. Water to Wine	John 2:1-11	• Jesus has God's power to do miracles.	Believe that God sent Jesus.	John 2:11
	2. Calming the Storm	Luke 8:22-25	• Jesus has power over nature.	Trust in Jesus' power when I am afraid.	Luke 8:25
	3. Walking on Water	Matthew 14:22-33	• Jesus is God's Son.	Keep my eyes on Jesus.	Matthew 14:33
	4. Healing a Paralytic	Mark 2:1-12	• Jesus has power over disease.	Act on my faith.	James 2:18
	5. Raising the Dead	Luke 8:40-42, 49-56	• Jesus has power over death.	Put my faith in Jesus.	Luke 18:27
	6. Jesus Appears to Thomas	John 20:30-31	• Jesus can do all things.	Pray to Jesus about everything.	John 20:31
21. Choose Your Character	1. Jesus in the Temple	Luke 2:41-52	• Jesus loved God.	I want to love the church like Jesus did.	Luke 2:47
	2. Mary and Martha	Luke 10:38-42	• Focus on people vs. things	When I make time for Jesus, he helps us get other things done.	Luke 10:42
	3. Saul and Samuel	1 Samuel 15	• Loving truth	Love to tell the truth.	Proverbs 17:20
	4. David and Jonathan	1 Samuel 20	• Best friends in the church	My friends should help me find strength in God.	1 Samuel 20:17 (NIRV)
	5. Tabitha (Dorcas)	Acts 9:36-43	• Giving and serving	Give and serve others.	Acts 9:36
	6. Lydia	Acts 16:11-15	• Eager and full of gratitude	Express my desire to learn and grow.	Acts 16:14
	7. Daniel	Daniel 1	• Pleasing God vs. pleasing people	When we do what pleases God, he will take care of us.	1 Thessalonians 2:4
	8. Review	Unit Review	• Imitating God	The Bible teaches me how to be godly.	Review

Resources

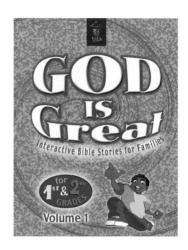

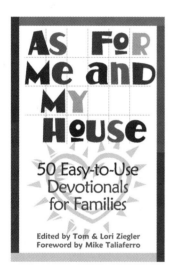

(888) DPI-BOOK

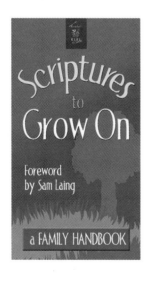

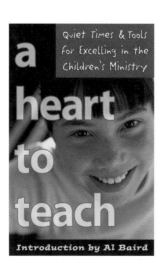

Visit Our Web Site at dpibooks.org